BETTER BY DESIGN

SHAPING THE BRITISH AIRWAYS BRAND

Paul Jarvis

In association with **BRITISH AIRWAYS**

AMBERLEY

First published 2015

Amberley Publishing
The Hill, Stroud
Gloucestershire, GL5 4EP

www.amberley-books.com

Copyright © Paul Jarvis & British Airways, 2015

The right of Paul Jarvis & British Airways to be identified as the Author of this work
has been asserted in accordance with the Copyrights, Designs and Patents Act 1988.

ISBN 978 1 4456 4283 3 (paperback)
ISBN 978 1 4456 4296 3 (ebook)

British Library Cataloguing in Publication Data.
A catalogue record for this book is available from the British Library.

Typesetting by Amberley Publishing.
Printed in the UK.

CONTENTS

FOREWORD

This book is exceptionally timely. Though the author was unaware when he finished his manuscript, British Airways has been selected as the consumer Superbrand of 2015. This holy grail of the brand and marketing worlds has traditionally been the preserve of huge global presences such as Apple, Rolex, Microsoft and Coca-Cola. So for our airline to take the prize for the second consecutive year is a remarkable achievement and completely without precedent in the travel industry.

What makes up our brand? There are three essential ingredients: British style, thoughtful service and flying know-how. This book outlines the development of each of those factors in the forty years that have passed since the British Overseas Airways Corporation (long-haul) and British European Airways (short-haul) were combined as a single entity, British Airways.

British style is ever present – from the earliest days of Concorde to the elegant cabins of our Airbus A380s today. Thoughtful service has evolved enormously as our cabin crew and customer service colleagues have successfully managed the revolution in customer tastes and expectations that has accompanied the transformation of air travel from luxury for the elite few to an experience afforded and enjoyed by tens of millions in a highly competitive industry.

And flying know-how underpins everything we do. A rich variety of aircraft types has passed through our hangars in forty years, and our pilots and engineers have shown themselves to be experts in every aspect of their operation.

We fly to all corners of the globe in all conditions, serving families, friends and businesses. To Fly. To Serve. That is the British Airways brand promise. This book tells the story of how promotion of our brand has changed over the decades. The promise itself remains constant.

Keith Williams
Executive Chairman, British Airways

ACKNOWLEDGEMENTS

When British Airways was voted the 2014 British Consumer Superbrand it rather set the seal on an earlier idea to write down what has shaped the British Airways brand since the company's formation in 1974. The idea had formed during the writing of an earlier book, *British Airways: An Illustrated History*, published by Amberley in April 2014. That book charted the path of British Airways and its predecessor airlines, but its ninety-five years of history inevitably meant a lot had to be left unsaid in a slim volume. In particular, it only scratched the surface of what the British Airways brand represented and how it had developed.

Going back ninety-five years, however, risked confusing two quite different civil aviation periods from a brand perspective, the 1920s and '30s pre-Second World War period being a quite separate commercial world and a book in itself. It was the post-war late 1940s and '50s that not only set the foundations for the framework of modern civil aviation but also saw the development of the brand values of British Airways' predecessor airlines, BOAC and BEA. They sought to meet the demands and challenges of the rapid growth of consumerism and what became cut-throat competition in the airline business, along the way creating their own brand promises and values that customers came to know, trust and expect. Following their merger to form British Airways, BOAC and BEA's experiences shaped the early development of the British Airways brand as it built its own brand values, which are encapsulated quite simply in its enduring promise, 'To Fly. To Serve.' It is the story of this period, from 1946 to 2014, that is the subject of this new book.

The underlying brand messages and products have certainly changed over the last seventy years, not least driven by technology and changing trends in design, style and ever-growing customer expectations, but there is not a great deal of difference between the advertised 'courtesy, service and flying skill' of the 1940s and the 'British style, thoughtful service and flying know-how' of today. What is very different, however, is the delivery of those brand expectations of trust, reliability and overall value that make up the British Airways brand promise – 'To Fly. To Serve.' – each and every time.

Trust, reliability and overall value rather sums up the contribution of the team of volunteers at the British Airways Heritage Collection, without whom the Collection could not exist. They make a substantial contribution towards supporting British Airways' business, in making a collection of national importance available to anyone who wishes to visit. Researchers, students, groups and individuals – all are welcome to visit at British Airways' headquarters building at Harmondsworth, near Heathrow Airport.

In writing this book my thanks go to all the Collection's volunteers for their overall support in putting it together and, in particular, Jim Davies and Bryan Jacques for their suggestions and diligent proofreading, Christine Quick and Adrian Constable for their patience and skill in producing the many images, and Alan Cavender and Barbara Wiltshire for keeping me on the straight and narrow of the task in hand.

Paul Jarvis
British Airways Heritage Collection

THE JOURNEY

Forty years is a long time in civil aviation. Since British Airways was formed in 1974 not only has aircraft technology rapidly changed, but many of the traditional commercial constraints that governed how airlines went about their business have evolved. In British Airways' case, an additional and major constraint was being the nationalised airline of the UK, a constraint removed in January 1987, when it was privatised.

The civil aviation business is, understandably, still closely regulated from a technical and operational perspective, but airlines today operate with considerable commercial freedom to promote their services to prospective customers. In a sense, airline services are no different from the provision of any other consumer services, and competition between airlines is now often encouraged by many governments, especially in the European Union and North America. The major airlines are certainly important contributors to national economies in a variety of ways, and what commercial regulations still exist are generally aimed at the application of competition legislation and the protection of consumers.

In what has become a highly competitive aviation environment in the last forty years, gaining an advantage is now about brand identity and the values that identity represents; it is an overall promise that creates an expectation, and achieving that time and time again makes for a successful airline, although not necessarily a great airline.

Airlines are competitive and complex businesses, and great airlines don't just happen. It is a long journey from formation through continuous improvement to operational excellence and outstanding service. Very few make it. In British Airways' case, it is many millions of journeys, each one a journey of customer expectations, experiences and emotions connected by tradition, innovation and service. Every detail of that customer experience, from first impressions to final destination, informs and shapes that journey. Above all, consistently exceptional service must be delivered, a service that customers know, recognise and expect. It is the promise to perform and deliver each and every time that is at the heart of any journey. It is that which makes a great airline and has made British Airways into one of the world's great brands.

This book is about the milestones on those millions of journeys that have shaped British Airways' identity in the last forty years. It is also about what makes the brand so distinctive. The name alone stands alongside the great consumer brands and represents British style, thoughtful service and flying know-how – three distinctive pillars that provide the foundation for the British Airways brand promise to deliver each and every time.

It is interesting to look back and see how airlines promoted themselves in earlier decades – they were shaped by the standards and aspirations of the age and society generally. In the immediate post-Second World War period this was about shaping a brand by advertising and marketing rather than by customer experience – the latter would come later, although operational skill was a key message in the early days. Advertising was about developing a standard and a style, an identity that was synonymous with the airline and its promise to perform. In the

Above: Creating a distinctive identity, or 'house style' as it was called, was an important early task for British Airways' predecessor airlines, BOAC and BEA, as civil aviation restarted in January 1946, following the ending of the Second World War just four months earlier. Both had their own logos: BOAC the 'Speedbird', designed by Theyre Lee-Elliott in 1932 and inherited from BOAC's predecessor airline Imperial Airways; BEA had the 'Keyline', designed by the advertising agency Colman, Prentis and Varley in 1946 and based on BEA's heraldic coat of arms and accompanying motto 'Clavis Europa', the 'Key to Europe'. They were clear identifiers of both companies and widely used in advertising and across both companies' assets, such as aircraft, vehicles and buildings. The concept of BOAC and BEA as 'brands' in themselves did not appear to have been in anyone's imagination, probably because the idea was 'too American' in the 1940s. That would change in later decades, but in their early years the two companies very much focussed on the simple concept of ensuring that they were known in the marketplace and that their names and logos were prominent.

Right: The Chatham Flag livery designed in 1997 for British Airways by the Admiral's Original Flag Loft in Chatham, Kent. It is a representation of the Union Flag of Great Britain and Northern Ireland that was itself designed in 1801 to represent the union of England, Scotland and Ireland by incorporating the three crosses of St George, St Andrew and St Patrick.

The Chatham Flag is painted on the tailfins of all British Airways aircraft and continues a long tradition of incorporating elements of the Union Flag within the design of the airline's earlier liveries and those of its predecessor airlines. It is a key element of the British Airways masterbrand.

ADMIRAL'S ORIGINAL FLAG LOFT
Flag-Makers. Chatham Historic Dockyard. England.

The Admiral's Original Flag Loft in Chatham, Kent, is the oldest in the UK, and has been making flags for more than 400 years. It was here that Nelson's famous signal flags ("England expects that every man will do his duty...") were made in 1805 before the Battle of Trafalgar, and this unique company still undertakes commissions for the Admiralty today. The Union Flag was created in 1801 to represent the union of England, Scotland and Ireland by incorporating the three crosses of St George, St Andrew and St Patrick. With its simple, graphic design, it is immediately recognisable as the symbol of the United Kingdom.

THE AIRCRAFT FLEET WILL BE THE MOST VISIBLE EXPRESSION OF THE NEW BRITISH AIRWAYS. BUT THE INCORPORATION OF WORLD IMAGES FROM CULTURES AND COMMUNITIES AROUND THE WORLD GOES MUCH MUCH FURTHER THAN ARTISTIC PAINTWORK. IT IS ABOUT APPRECIATING VIEWS, NEEDS AND EXPECTATIONS. IT IS ABOUT RECOGNISING AND RESPECTING DIFFERENCES, ABOUT UNDERSTANDING PEOPLE, THEIR LIKES AND DISLIKES. IT IS ALSO ABOUT PUTTING SOMETHING BACK, ABOUT CARING FOR THE ENVIRONMENT AND SUPPORTING POSITIVE PROJECTS BY CONTRIBUTING TIME, MONEY AND EXPERTISE. IN A TIME WHEN AIR TRAVEL HAS CHANGED FROM BEING EXTRAORDINARY TO BEING PART OF EVERYDAY LIFE, BRITISH AIRWAYS HAS EVOLVED AND RESPONDED: BY LISTENING TO PEOPLE, THROUGH INVESTMENT IN THE LATEST TECHNOLOGY AND BY LOOKING TO THE FUTURE. THIS EVOLUTION WILL CONTINUE, THE AIRLINE WILL GROW AND, OVER THE YEARS, CHANGE. BUT IT WILL ALWAYS BE BOUND BY ITS CORE PHILOSOPHY: TO REMAIN THE WORLD'S FAVOURITE AIRLINE.

PRODUCED BY THE HIGH LIFE TEAM, PREMIER MAGAZINES LTD, HAYMARKET HOUSE, 1 OXENDON STREET, LONDON, SW1Y 4EE TEL: 0171 925 2544 FAX: 0171 839 4508

immediate years after the Second World War many standards were quite basic compared to today, but circumstances and people's expectations were less demanding. It was very much about getting from A to B at a price one could afford, and even the rich and famous were limited by what was on offer or possible. Looking back gives an impression of a rapidly changing world, and the standards of today can be judged by this progression.

British Airways also has a first-class pedigree to judge by. Its predecessor nationalised airlines – British Overseas Airways Corporation (BOAC) and British European Airways (BEA) set the standards of the decades from the 1940s to the 1970s, when they were merged to form British Airways in 1974. That period, from the end of the Second World War in August 1945, represents a time when civil aviation moved from the certainties of regulatory protection in the 1940s and '50s, to the stirrings of mass air travel in the 1960s and '70s, to full-blown competition in the 1980s and beyond. The 1970s were the real catalyst for change as competition between airlines began to be encouraged, firstly by the US and UK governments, then by the EEC, now the European Union, in the late 1980s. British Airways' formation on 1 April 1974 meant the company was launched into what was becoming a brave new aviation world. If it were to succeed it would need to rapidly make a name for itself and begin to stand out in an already crowded aviation sky.

BOAC's early media advertisements were often quite basic, with an exotic touch reflecting the destination, and were possibly due to the influence of F. H. K. Henrion, who was a design consultant to BOAC's newly formed design committee. In a way, BOAC did not have to try too hard to attract business as they had few, if any, direct competitors on many of the old British Empire routes. Even in later years, as many empire countries became independent, BOAC still benefited as there were large volumes of UK government administrators and their families continuing to travel to and from the UK. The early aircraft were not large and BOAC was very short of them, so it did not take much to fill them up.

BEA's advertisements were more down to earth – promoting the existence of a route network in war-torn Europe and the experience of their air crews in getting passengers from A to B safely was more important for BEA in these early years. Interestingly, BEA used Stuart Advertising Agency, the premier UK advertising agency in the 1930s that had been used by BOAC's predecessor companies Imperial Airways and British Airways Ltd, the latter a private airline taken over by the UK government in 1939 and merged with Imperial Airways to form BOAC. Stuart's reused a late 1930s British Airways Ltd strapline, 'As the crow flies – only faster', for BEA as one of its first simple advertisements, a make-do-and-mend approach reflecting the austerity of the post-war 1940s. (Above: Stuart Advertising Agency, right: Theyre Lee-Elliott)

Looking back, the travel aspirations of customers were also changing in the 1970s. The 1960s Mediterranean sun spots were starting to lose their attraction as long-haul destinations became affordable for many people. Low advance booking fares had been pioneered by BOAC and, unsurprisingly, Jamaican beaches and African safaris became more alluring than Rimini or the Costa del Sol. The few extra flying hours to New York were also a small price to pay for a visit to the 'Big Apple'. New York had long overtaken Paris as the city destination of choice for the wealthy and famous, and now it was becoming available to almost anyone.

This was indeed a brave new aviation world, a world that was very new territory for many airlines that had previously all charged broadly the same fares and were heavily restricted, by industry agreements and an arcane government approval process, on the level of on-board service each could offer. BOAC's customer promise was to provide matchless on-board comfort, a promise that had been limited in scope and value due to those industry restrictions. All that could be done, other than in first class, was to attempt to provide an overall customer experience that would make BOAC stand out from the crowd. As the industry restrictions gradually fell away in the later 1970s and early '80s, it was left to British Airways to develop its own individual style and promise to perform. This new freedom to innovate was certainly helped by the introduction of the Boeing 747 in the early 1970s and, later, the Lockheed TriStar-1. The huge size of these 'next generation' commercial jet aircraft was to open up a new world of possibilities that airlines could offer to their customers.

This spread: BOAC's 'Speedbird' logo was even incorporated into the design of the concrete side arches above its new engineering maintenance hangar opened in 1954 at London Heathrow Airport, and can be seen there to this day. The huge hangar itself represented the emergence of a new, modern world order, design- and technology-led, in which everyone would benefit, not just a select few. It was the beginning of a new consumer-led society that would blossom in the next decade and eventually cause the full force of competition to be thrust upon the commercial aviation world in the 1970s.

The 'Speedbird' was part of a consistent approach by BOAC's design committee to 'harmonise the manifold activities of BOAC into a characteristic "style" which will be representative of the best British design and workmanship and which will create prestige both for the corporation and Great Britain throughout the world'. What both BOAC and BEA really wanted was to be identified as part of the emerging new, modern world order. Aviation would play a key part in its development as trade and commerce began rapidly to develop once again between Great Britain and the rest of the world. Both airlines would benefit enormously from that, although their respective markets and opportunities were markedly different and would eventually need different approaches.

Fly British everywhere

British flying skill

all the way

Fly to London—and thence to all parts of the world by the British Airways. All along this great network of air routes you are flown by British crews, unsurpassed in skill and experience. You travel in perfect comfort — and everywhere you go you meet traditional British courtesy, the same high standards of service.

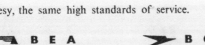

BEA   BOAC

BRITISH EUROPEAN OVERSEAS AIRWAYS

The 'Speedbird' logo was also prominently shown on BOAC's aircraft. This one is a Lockheed Constellation 049, an American aircraft and one of five that BOAC had initially been allowed by the UK government to purchase in 1946 to use on UK–US routes. The UK had a 'Buy British' policy for its nationalised airlines, but there were no suitable UK-built aircraft to allow BOAC to compete against the large US airlines Pan American, Trans World and American Overseas. They also had much bigger fleets, so it was a very uneven match for several years and, of course, it was highly competitive. BOAC had to try very much harder on UK–US routes to attract business and its early advertisements reflected this, highlighting 'British' style, courtesy and the experience of its crews, all attributes attractive to American consumers which have stood the test of time.

The 'Speedbird' as a brand 'mark' was also much more appreciated in the USA and widely used in association with the initials 'B.O.A.C'. It became an enduring and recognisable symbol clearly associated with BOAC and would eventually be classified as one of the most successful brand marks of the twentieth century.

BEA's 'Keyline' logo was distinctive enough but did not really stand out on the unpainted, silver aircraft fuselages of the time. It is only just visible on the nose of the BEA DC3 being refuelled at Northolt Airport, their main base, in the late 1940s. It was also never that prominent in BEA's advertising, and over time often took second place to the initials 'BEA'. The use of BEA's name without the logo became the norm by the late 1950s, when a new design incorporating the initials 'BEA' in a distinctive red or black square was created by the UK designer Mary De Saulles, and the 'Keyline' was consigned to history. (Far right: Andre Amstutz)

AUSTRIA
SWITZERLAND
ITALY
FRANCE
SPAIN
SWEDEN
NORWAY
GERMANY

BRITISH EUROPEAN AIRWAYS

fly BEA
to a paradise of sun and snow

BRITISH EUROPEAN AIRWAYS

This is *your* business, Sir...

We of the three great British air corporations can help you to expand your business. With 190,000 miles of route, flown by the world's most experienced airmen, we offer you quick and comfortable travel to all parts of the world . . . . .

You may have difficulty these days with material, staff or plant shortages, but there is always an outlet for initiative in the imaginative use of air travel. It's the personal contact that counts, whether your customer is in Rome or Rio.

Fly British yourself — make your executives fly — send your freight by air. That's where the business of the future lies.

BEA between the principal cities of Britain, and from London to the principal cities of Europe. B.O.A.C. and associated companies link Britain with the USA, the British Commonwealth and the Far East. B.S.A.A. links Britain with South America and the West Indies.

BRITISH OVERSEAS EUROPEAN S.AMERICAN **AIRWAYS**

mean business

Fly British everywhere and

experience **Britain's welcome**

the moment you step aboard

Fly to London, to the centre of the British Airways system which covers the world. A British welcome greets you as soon as you step aboard the aircraft. And everywhere along these BEA and BOAC routes you enjoy traditional courtesy and superlative service. You fly swiftly, in perfect comfort and are flown by superbly skilled British crews.

 B E A    **B O A C**

BRITISH EUROPEAN OVERSEAS **AIRWAYS**

SOLPLASSEN I, OSLO.   TEL: 42.36.96 & 42.37.02.

TO LONDON
in luxury

The London Policeman is a symbol of courtesy
and service. The same helpfulness is with
you when you fly to London by
British European Airways.

RESERVATIONS :

*Leading Travel Agents (no booking fee) and at BEA office,
Solplassen 1, Oslo. Tel: 42.36.96 & 42.37.02.*

Connexions from London to all parts of the world by BOAC and BSAA

BEA
BRITISH EUROPEAN AIRWAYS

BRITISH EUROPEAN AIRWAYS
ROOMY INTERIOR OF BEA DOUGLAS AIRLINE

This spread: Promotional activity in the austere years following the Second World War was
often done jointly by BOAC and BEA, together with the third UK nationalised airline of the
time, British South American Airways (BSAA). This not only saved money but also helped to
sell to passengers travelling between Europe, BEA's principal route network, and the rest of
the world via London, BOAC's and BSAA's networks. As the UK's three nationalised airlines,
their primary role was more about promoting Britain and trade for British companies rather
than achieving a profit for the UK Treasury. In their joint advertising the airlines often used
the abbreviated collective name 'British Airways', and highlighted what were seen as positive
'British' attributes such as courtesy and service coupled with the airlines' undoubted flying
skills. The London policeman cartoon character was also widely used as a recognised symbol of
courtesy and service, the same level of helpful service passengers could expect on board. Apart
from this there was very little 'product' advertising in these very early years, mainly because
there was very little product; cabin interiors and seating standards being quite basic by today's
standards, although they were sometimes advertised as 'luxury'.

Top left and bottom left: Make do and mend was the necessary approach to BEA's promotion at the 1946 Brussels Aeronautical Show. With many materials in very short supply at the end of the Second World War, Brussels itself having only been liberated two years earlier, it was all about making do with what could be found. A trestle table, a British civil air ensign flag and some display boards for adverts and photographs would grace any village fete today. Things were a bit better at the Paris Aeronautical Show, also in 1946, with a more modern stand, although the uniforms of the stewardesses – BOAC (front row), BEA (middle row) and BSAA (back row) – are still very formal, wartime vintage.

Above and opposite: By 1947, with the improving supply of materials and more time to design a modern display, BOAC's futuristic stand at the Blackpool Publicity Exhibition compares well even with today's exhibition standards. Both BOAC and BEA frequently took stands at major exhibitions in the UK and overseas well into the 1950s. The 1951 Festival of Britain on London's South Bank could not be missed and was widely advertised abroad. BEA's Spanish advert placed in the Madrid media and showing the iconic Festival logo, designed by Abram Games, is a good example. BOAC even took a full-page poster for its overseas advertising. (Far right: Abram Games)

Vaya por aire al

Festival de Inglaterra

en un avión inglés

MADRID-LONDRES-LOS CINCO CONTINENTES				
MADRID-BURDEOS			MADRID-GIBRALTAR	
Todos los días				
08 00	sal.	Gibraltar	lleg.	17 25
09 55	lleg.	Madrid	sal.	15 25
10 40	sal.	Madrid	lleg.	14 25
12 50	lleg.	Burdeos	sal.	12 15
13 50	sal.	Burdeos	lleg.	11 35
16 45	lleg.	Londres	sal.	08 40

También servicios desde
Barcelona a Londres.

Enlaces en Londres para todo el Mundo por B.O.A.C.

Reservas: En los principales Agentes de
Viajes (sin recargo) y en las Oficinas de
BEA, Avenida de José Antonio 68,
Madrid. Tel: 21.10.60.

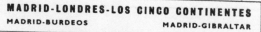

Líneas Aéreas Británicas

For very particular people

THE Monarch

direct between London and New York

LONDON

LONDON has for centuries been a world centre of finance, commerce and entertainment and its attractions, above all the unique ceremonial of Royal Occasions, present an unrivalled year-round programme of events.

NEW YORK

NEW YORK is a city of boundless vitality, where everything seems bigger, taller, newer, faster, busier and more exciting than almost anywhere on earth. You'll find entertainment and hospitality unlimited.

ELEGANCE, LUXURY AND IMPECCABLE SERVICE – these are the keynotes when you travel by "The Monarch," the B.O.A.C. de luxe Service flying overnight direct between London and New York. You fly in a magnificent double-decked Stratocruiser – so spacious, with its lower-deck bar lounge, sleeper accommodation and luxurious dressing rooms, that it seems like a flying hotel. Only the very best is good enough aboard "The Monarch" and by limiting the number carried, B.O.A.C. offers each passenger extra spacious comfort, extra personal attention – yet there's no surcharge when you fly by "The Monarch"! Whether on business or pleasure-bound, you will appreciate not only the convenient frequency of the Services, but the joy of a journey giving the utmost rest and relaxation. You arrive on the other side of the Atlantic feeling completely refreshed, ready for the urgent business problem, the important conference or the social pleasures of your visit. When making your reservation to the U.S.A., remember you can book right through to destinations in all parts of North America, travelling by "The Monarch" to New York and completing your journey on the same ticket by domestic airlines. Corresponding facilities are available from New York to points throughout Europe and the Eastern Hemisphere. You fly by "The Monarch" to London, where conveniently timed air connections can be made: by British European Airways or other airlines to all the principal cities of Europe; by B.O.A.C. to Africa, the Middle East, Pakistan, India, Ceylon, the Far East and Australasia.

FLY THERE BY

B·O·A·C

THE FIRST AIRLINE TO FLY THE NORTH ATLANTIC AS A TWO-WAY YEAR-ROUND SERVICE

During the early 1950s, new, modern aircraft joined the fleets of both BOAC and BEA. They gave the opportunity for both airlines to develop their own distinctive on-board services and products, e.g. BOAC's 'Monarch' service on its North Atlantic routes and 'Majestic' service elsewhere, BEA's 'Silver Wing' service on its London–Paris route. These were all one-class services, effectively a first-class level of service, until 1952, when lower 'Tourist' fares were introduced. Tourist was a second-class service, a product BOAC called the 'Coronet' service to give it a more upmarket name. (Above: Adelman)

To walk into the sumptuous lower-deck lounge is to feel at once the honoured guest of an exclusive international club.

TAKES GOOD CARE OF YOU

Above left: The Coronet service was a good indication of the restrictions imposed on airlines that were members of the airline industry trade association (IATA), effectively limiting competition between them. BOAC and BEA were both members, so were heavily restricted on what they could offer their Tourist customers, e.g. no free alcoholic drinks, cigarettes or cigars and a strict limit on the meal content and seat pitch (the distance between a seat and the one in front of it). In this picture, although the stewardess is handing around a bowl of fruit, only one piece per passenger was the internationally agreed rule. The rest of the meal also looks rather colourless and basic and is, presumably, breakfast.

Above middle and right: By contrast, BOAC's Monarch first-class customers on their luxury Stratocruiser aircraft had no on-board service limitations. They even had a lower-deck club lounge to relax in and enjoy a free canapé and cocktail while awaiting the preparation of a personally served dinner of Turtle Soup Royale followed by Filet Mignon and fine wines.

Announcing
BEA
SILVER WING

A new Luxury Service between London and Paris

From June 16th, ELIZABETHAN airliners of BEA's SILVER WING service will leave London Airport for Paris every day at 1.00 p.m., arriving at Le Bourget at 2.25 p.m. Aboard, an excellent lunch—the *only* hot lunch served on any daily air service to Paris—will be offered, with BEA's compliments, Moët et Chandon *special cuvée* champagne is also included. This is the most luxurious of all daily services between the two capitals.

Yet the fare remains the same: just the normal £15.19.0 return. (Remember there are also excursion returns to Paris at £12.15.0 and £10.10.0.)

For bookings and information apply to your Travel Agent, BEA Offices or BEA, Dorland Hall, Regent Street, London, S.W.1. (GERrard 9833).

BRITISH   EUROPEAN   AIRWAYS

fly BEA

by VISCOUNT to Switzerland and the Mediterranean — at the new low fares!

To fly aboard BEA's pressurized, turbo-prop VISCOUNT (BEA 'Discovery' Class) is a wonderful experience. The perfect ease of its flight, the stillness, the smoothness, the feeling at the end of the longest journey of quiet and restfulness—all this is altogether new.

The Viscount flies more smoothly and quietly because it is powered by four Rolls-Royce Dart jet propeller-turbines. These draw in a great force of air, compress it, mix it with fuel, and burn it. The high energy gas jets thus released drive the turbines which, in turn, drive the propellers.

VISCOUNT
BEA 'DISCOVERY' CLASS

world's first **TURBO-PROP** airliner

BRITISH   EUROPEAN   AIRWAYS

BEA's 'Silver Wing' service was a similarly relaxed affair, and used its new Airspeed Ambassador aircraft. On the short Paris route, the midday flight time was even extended by ten minutes to allow for a more leisurely lunch. At other times of the day, a cup of tea and a sandwich was quite acceptable, particularly if it came with a cheerful BEA stewardess to offer that understated 'British' style of service to make one feel at home. BEA named its aircraft fleets by class, for example the Ambassador was the 'Elizabethan Class' and the Viscount the 'Discovery Class', and these were often referred to in advertising. By today's standards these were brand names in themselves, but were never referred to as such.

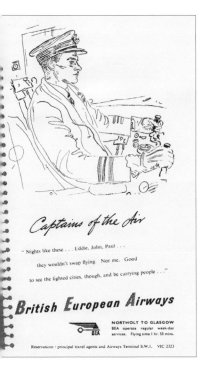

Captains of the Air

" Nights like these . . . Eddie, John, Paul . . .

they wouldn't swap flying. Nor me. Good

to see the lighted cities, though, and be carrying people . . ."

British European Airways

NORTHOLT TO GLASGOW
BEA operate regular week-day
services. Flying time 1 hr. 55 mins.

Reservation : principal travel agents and Airways Terminal S.W.1.   VIC 2323

B·O·A·C takes good care of you

B.O.A.C. WAS THE FIRST AIRLINE to operate a two-way, year-round passenger air service across the North Atlantic and 1957 sees the completion of 20 years of Transatlantic flight operations. Long experience makes B.O.A.C. Captains and crews the most skilled and reliable in the world and has given B.O.A.C. a reputation second to none for superb service in the air.

Now, with the introduction of DC-7Cs into B.O.A.C.'s Transatlantic Fleet, you enjoy this unsurpassed service and experience while flying in one of the world's newest, fastest and most comfortable airliners. The latest of a long line of famous piston-engined aircraft produced by the Douglas Aircraft Company, the DC-7C is not only faster, quieter and longer-ranged than its predecessors, but incorporates a whole host of improvements increasing both passenger comfort and operational efficiency.

When you fly B.O.A.C. by DC-7C, you enjoy the *finest* service in the *fastest* airliner across the Atlantic.

B·O·A·C TAKES GOOD CARE OF YOU

The introduction of Tourist fares gave both BOAC and BEA a much-needed opportunity to promote their respective services. The newer aircraft joining their fleets were larger, faster and of longer range, and needed to be filled. There was a huge untapped potential, certainly in the rapidly developing US and European consumer markets, to encourage people to travel abroad. With more foreign airlines having started operating since the late 1940s, however, competition was intensifying and even BOAC with its traditional markets had to try harder. Although most airlines charged the same fares on each route, there were marked differences in their standards of reliability and level of service. Both BOAC and BEA could take advantage of this. As the nationalised airlines of the UK they were seen as safe, reliable and hugely experienced, and the service was pretty good too. The experience of their crews was often used as a major advertising feature; BEA, rather surprisingly, continued to use their pilots' wartime experience as an advertising feature for some years. BOAC was rather more subtle about it.

fly **BEA**

ZURICH

BRITISH EUROPEAN AIRWAYS

fly **BEA** to **VENICE**

FOR CORTINA AND THE
DOLOMITES

BRITISH EUROPEAN AIRWAYS

Apart from promoting their on-board services, both BOAC and BEA often focussed on destination advertising in their early years. Even as late as the 1950s, hand-painted posters were still being used, but were rapidly being overtaken by photographic works. BEA used a range of artists to encourage travel to iconic, upmarket destinations like the Swiss lakes, but at the same time used photographers, as shown in the almost 1930s-style poster, to promote skiing in the Italian Alps. Sun, sea, sand and now skiing were growing contributors to BEA's original promise to be the 'Key to Europe'. Growth in its passenger numbers would make it the seventh-largest airline in the world by 1951, measured by passengers carried, and eventually it would claim to be 'No. 1 in Europe'.

Above left: BEA's passengers were hard won, however, and reflected a clear difference between BOAC and BEA in the value of their respective markets. BEA's passengers were very seasonal, with the vast majority being holidaymakers travelling on its southern European routes. A mass consumer market was rapidly emerging, encouraged by innovative destination- and price-led promotions wrapping inclusive, affordable air travel and hotel packages into glossy tour brochures. With packages easy to buy using new airline credit schemes that were easy to use, almost nothing had to be done other than choose where to go. 'Fun, Sun and BEA' flying to Venice for fourteen days, half board, at under £49 was a very good deal for the customer but had low margins for the airline.

Above right and opposite: BEA's 'Silver Wing' service reputation had also been linked to the upmarket 'Club Méditerranée' brand and the growing market for young people looking for a more exciting beach holiday. BEA knew, however, that it needed a stronger and more distinctive brand image if it was to keep up or be ahead of the game. 'BEA' as a word mark and especially the 'Keyline' logo were rapidly becoming unidentifiable in the growing plethora of brightly lit high-street shop signs. The result, by the designer Mary de Saulles, was the BEA 'Red Square' design. Created in the late 1950s, it was ahead of its time and very much 'a sign of the '60s', and it certainly made BEA stand out from the crowd. Often used in a template form, designed by Mary de Saulles to provide a standard header and footer so that when repeated in rows or pairs it gave a greater impact to the whole design, it was a feature unique to BEA's advertising of the time. (Opposite, first three: S. Barany, far right: S. Jeffreys)

The much higher cost of BOAC's long-haul travel inevitably played to a narrower audience who could afford what were still high prices for even the 'Coronet' second-class services, let alone the premium products such as 'Monarch' or 'Majestic'. Lower prices were, however, slowly being introduced as cheaper 'Economy' fares, and other special fares such as 'Excursion' fares and discounted group fares began to be developed in the later 1950s.

fly B·O·A·C

to the Caribbean

fly B·O·A·C

to the Middle East

Above: BOAC had a much wider choice of exotic destinations to entice customers with than BEA. The more traditional delights of the tropics and the excitement of the Middle East were unknown worlds to the majority of US and European consumers in the 1950s unless they were wealthy and well travelled. If finance was a problem, then the airlines had even devised low-cost travel plans. Place a deposit and pay off the rest later. The world of air travel was rapidly moving towards a way of life recognisable to many people today.

Right: The succeeding 1960s saw the beginning of modern, price-led advertising. Cabin differentiation was by fare type, and with only two cabins everyone other than those in first class got the same economy service at the back end of the aircraft, no matter what they had paid. This would eventually cause complaints from those passengers paying higher fares than the others sitting alongside them in the same cabin, for example business passengers paying the full economy fare. By the late 1970s, this state of affairs would lead to British Airways introducing an 'Executive' cabin for full-fare economy passengers that eventually became the 'Club' cabin, a unique concept and a key product of today's British Airways.

Will the passenger who has paid full fare please come forward.

A forward cabin on all 747s* is now reserved for passengers paying the normal Economy Class fare.

At first sight, our new Executive Cabin won't seem dramatically different from the rest of the Economy Class of our 747s.

But when you travel in it, the difference will become very apparent. For this cabin has been reserved for those who have paid the normal Economy Class fare.

As well as being separated from the other passengers, you'll enjoy a number of little touches designed to make you feel more comfortable.

You'll also find there is no movie show to interrupt your work or your reading.

And as a parting bonus, you'll normally be able to leave the aircraft ahead of the rest of the Economy Class passengers.

If you would like to travel in this special cabin, be sure to say so when you make your reservation.

And please check-in early. Our Executive Cabin seats only 48.

"It's nice to have you with us."

*This facility is not available on London Chicago London services.

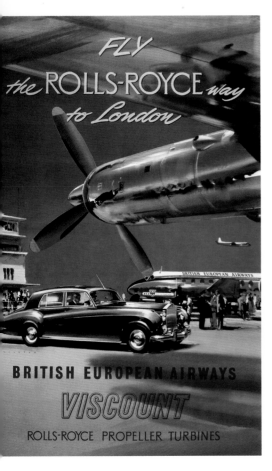

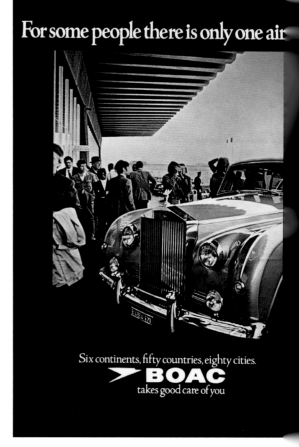

The 1960s were also the beginning of the new jet age. BOAC had been the launch customer for the Comet 4 passenger jet aircraft in 1958 on the North Atlantic, but within weeks Boeing had introduced the 707. If any jet aircraft was to define the 1960s, it would be the 707, and it was widely used by BOAC in its advertising as a plus point, together with a subtle hint of its reliability (and luxury), as BOAC used Rolls-Royce engines. The use of such engines gave BOAC and BEA (and subsequently British Airways) a powerful implied brand relationship over the decades, often used in advertising to suggest that for discerning owners of a Rolls-Royce motor car BOAC and BEA were the airlines of choice. (Above left: Frank Wootton)

Right: By the end of the 1960s BEA had changed its livery again. The red square had lasted ten years and was considered dated, losing out to new trends in graphic design that were weakening its visual impact and identity among a growing number of competing symbols. A simpler, more striking graphic was adopted, designed by Henrion Design Associates using a cut-out of part of the UK's Union Flag in a stylised 'flight' form and with BEA's initials re-styled and shown separately.

On paper the new name design worked in some ways, but it was the part-Union Flag displayed on the tailfins of BEA's aircraft that really stood out. Henrion believed the Union Flag should be an integral part of BEA's image to reflect its British traditions as one of the UK's nationalised airlines. Partly for similar reasons, it would eventually be incorporated into the tailfin design of British Airways' first livery in 1974.

Far right: BOAC had also reworked its 'Speedbird' logo and 'BOAC' name mark in the early 1960s. Redesigned by Karl Gerstner in 1964, it actually had not needed much change. Removing the full stops between the initials B.O.A.C and using a new block typeface made it a stronger image and more aligned to the bolder graphics of the time. The 'Speedbird' similarly was made broader and shown in a more consistent manner. Consistency of style, form and placement would in future underpin BOAC's brand presentation and begin the journey to the eventual development of 'British Airways' as a masterbrand in itself.

... the most comfortable economy class seat in the world ...

sitting pretty aboard the BOAC VC10

Top left and right: A serious rival to the 707 was the British-built Vickers VC10 aircraft. It could not quite match the 707's economic performance but more than made up for that in passenger appeal. This was BOAC's chance to stand out from the crowd, and it certainly made a glamorous attempt. Advertised as 'Swift, Silent, Serene' due to the engines being placed at the rear of the aircraft, it promised matchless comfort 'in the most comfortable economy class seat in the world'. Superior cabin style and comfort was one way to get around the industry agreements limiting what could be offered to economy passengers. A revolutionary new seat with facings by the British designer Robin Day increased legroom and gave more overall space. Although the industry rules limited the distance between economy seats, nothing was said about the design of the seat or the design of the aircraft cabin. This was an opportunity BOAC exploited to the full, with an interior design by Day's wife, the renowned interior designer Lucienne Day.

Bottom: For those passengers fortunate enough to be in the VC10's 'Monarch' first-class cabin, an even higher standard of comfort and catering was the expectation and the reality.

we'll give you 15 days in East Africa.

Take a BOAC Earthshrinker holiday for £153.

By the early 1970s, price innovation coupled with exotic destinations were encouraging more and more people to fly. BOAC's low-cost advance booking fares and inclusive tour holidays were packaged under the name 'Earthshrinkers'. The earth was certainly shrinking by the early 1970s as lower air fares began to encourage many people in the Western world to think globally when making their holiday travel plans. There was a widespread use of cartoon characters and graphics in the 1970s, a sort of 'pop art', extroverted approach following their use in commercial brand advertising from the 1960s onwards and instant appeal to the younger consumer. This was a particular target market for BOAC, with the expectation that it would be this consumer group with increasing disposable income that would be interested in travelling farther afield for their holidays.

The Earthshrinkers are here.

Now you and your money can go a long, long way.

Now's the time for that reunion in North America!

Grandchildren you've never even met?
Parents you haven't seen for years?
Invitations from friends all set with a big welcome?

Well, what are you waiting for?
Air fares to the USA and Canada are at their lowest level during the off-season months and BOAC offers the full range of excursion, group and charter fares.
Since these fares offer such big savings over the ordinary Economy Class fares, certain conditions have to be complied with. However, that's not a problem – just a question of careful planning.

This folder shows you, in brief, the range of BOAC's low rates across the North Atlantic and other folders are available giving full details of these and similar fares to points throughout North America, including Chicago, Detroit, Los Angeles, Miami, Philadelphia, Toronto, Vancouver, Washington.

Get in touch with BOAC or your Travel Agent now, tell them your travel requirements and ask them to quote you the lowest available fares.

Above: The increase in air travel worldwide during the later 1960s and early 1970s had bitten hard into the traditional shipping business and this encouraged the shipping companies to work with the airlines to develop joint products. BOAC had a number of deals with shipping companies including Cunard on the North Atlantic to New York and Chandris Cruises, among others, to the Caribbean.

Left: 'Earthshrinker' fares to the USA and Canada were also particularly attractive to families, many with relatives abroad whom they may not have seen for many years. Family reunions were a particular theme encouraged by the growing range of special fares with new advance booking conditions or other travel restrictions. The whole point for the airlines was to increase the numbers of passengers and increase revenue, even marginal revenue, by closely controlling the numbers of seats sold at these low fares, but making them sufficiently restrictive to discourage higher-fare paying passengers, often business passengers who needed more flexible travel arrangements, from trading down.

Fly-Cruise Winter holidays were a new idea that packaged the ease of flying in a few hours to the sunshine of the Caribbean and transferring to a luxury ship to cruise the islands. Chandris Cruises' passenger liner *Romanza* looks more 1930s than 1970s which, indeed, she was, having been built in 1939 and, after only one voyage, taken over by the German navy as a repair vessel during the Second World War. Looking outdated compared to the ultra-modern Caribbean cruise liners of later years, she nevertheless has an old-world charm about her that must have made such cruises very enjoyable for her passengers. BOAC's VC10 aircraft shown on the brochure cover flew passengers to Antigua to embark on the *Romanza* or her sister ship *Regina* for a fifteen-day cruise from £194 per person, all-inclusive.

Above and top left: In the mid-1970s the newly formed British Airways advertised the Lockheed TriStar-1 as 'the introduction of European space travel'. The size of the aircraft's cabin was a real improvement on previous commercial aircraft on European routes, which had only a single aisle and could make using the facilities during meal service a bit of a squeeze. Now cabins could be subdivided to make a more intimate, 'homely' space and allow the cabin crew to create a more personal, caring atmosphere. The TriStar-1 was even advertised as 'caring for people', both the operating crew and passengers, who both benefited from the more relaxed environment created by its large interior.

Bottom left: What was also changing as the 1970s evolved was the more relaxed dress style of passengers that was rapidly becoming the acceptable norm. Only a few years before, and even in the economy cabin, it was all rather formal mid-1960s chic, with passengers smartly dressed. Although in this BOAC 707 economy-class promotional image they were all actors and actresses dressed for the part, it was reflective of a now long-gone standard that presumed one dressed up, not down, to fly, even when going on holiday. How times have changed, and they were to change quickly as the 1970s got into its stride.

2

THE CHALLENGE AND THE PROMISE OF THE '70S

On its formation in 1974, British Airways was advertised as 'The best of BEA and BOAC'. As the UK's two nationalised airlines, they had benefitted from as good as a UK monopoly between the late 1940s and early 1960s. Both were well-respected airlines for their undoubted experience, reputation and products. They were respected both by their customers and even by their foreign rivals. BEA advertised itself as 'The No. 1 in Europe'; BOAC would 'Take good care of you'. The task facing British Airways was how to capture that respect and reputation and mould it into its own; in other words, how to take the best of each and make it better.

British Airways' first priority, however, was to make a name for itself in the marketplace. Its first advertising campaigns were targeted at the broader audience of prospective customers in order to let the public know who it was, where it had come from and what it had to offer. Subsequent campaigns targeted more specific customer groups and product offerings. One direct promise was 'We'll take more care of you', a play on the BOAC promise, but it would take a lot more than that to meet the challenge of the brave new aviation world. During the early years of British Airways, 'caring' was the central theme of a campaign that placed the concept at the heart of its customer focus. Headlined internally as 'The Challenge and the Promise', research had indicated that customers selected British Airways because it had a reputation for reliability and for understanding their needs. The company interpreted this as a reflection of its caring approach and its 'plus factor'; today we would call this its unique selling point. Overall, it was seen as service in its totality, as measured by 'punctuality, reliability, quality care for its customers' – in that sense a wider concept than just 'care' alone.

Management was also very clear about the challenges. Gerry Draper, British Airways' Director of Commercial Operations and a former BEA man, carefully used the term 'provided we stay in business'. This was a clear hint that staying in business was no longer guaranteed; British Airways was still the nationalised airline of the UK but others were coming up on the inside track, not least British Caledonian, the UK government's favoured 'second force' airline. British Airways could not afford to be complacent and management recognised that.

It seemed that not all staff saw this with the same degree of clarity. Many saw the company itself as the most important element, a nationalised 'family' too valuable to the UK economy to be allowed to fail. Although customer care was clearly important, and many staff tried hard to make it happen, it was not seen as central to the continuation of British Airways' existence as the flag carrier of the UK, a status some believed that the government would always support. This approach had to change. Management made the point that while the company was perceived as having some of the best staff in the business, the promise to 'take more care' would be meaningless unless everyone worked together as a team. Together, British Airways was clearly demonstrating to its customers that it really did care about not only their comfort but also their overall travel experience, and that promise was delivered each and every time.

London

> BOAC
British Airways

Earthshrinkers to USA and Canada

EFFECTIVE 15 APRIL 1973

> **BOAC**
British Airways

BEA

British Airways

to Greece and the Greek Islands

Non-stop from London to
Athens
Corfu
Heraklion
Rhodes
Salonica
Summer 1973

Now the world is yours

British airways

British airways
The best of BEA and BOAC

This spread: British Airways launched its very first UK advertising campaign on 17 September 1973, just over six months before opening for business on 1 April 1974, called 'Now the world is yours'. First impressions were seen as critical in 'attracting and keeping good customers', an important element being to promote the airline's heritage and the fact that it would be 'the best of BEA and BOAC'. Earlier in 1973 both BEA and BOAC had begun to introduce the name 'British Airways' into their promotional advertising as the first stage in making the public aware of the upcoming launch of a new airline. The campaign played to the new company's great strength in its large route network, the largest in the world, and its reputation (through BEA and BOAC) of reliability and personal service. Henry Marking, British Airways' first Group Managing Director, saw these elements as the hallmarks of 'not just a great airline, but also the best airline'. This was to be a further and significant stage in British Airways' journey to becoming a successful and a great airline, like its predecessors, but also to becoming the best airline. (Above: Foote, Cone & Belding, now DraftFCB London Ltd)

Gerry Draper had also made the point that it took far too long for new products to come to market. If British Airways was to fulfil its long-term plan to be carrying twice as many passengers in 1986 as it did in 1979, it would need to find products tailored to fit their differing needs. The 747 'Executive Cabin' had been introduced in 1977 to meet the needs of the full-fare economy passengers, essentially businessmen, and was a growing success. The major growth, however, was expected to be in the package holiday market, especially on long-haul routes, and the total market was expected to double to 6 million passengers by 1986. British Airways' Chief Executive, Roy Watts, saw those passengers as 'prepared to accept limited choice, high load factors, simple service, and very basic ground facilities in return for excellent value for money' – the sort of service the package holiday customer had traditionally been offered by tour operators to the Mediterranean in the 1960s. Whether the same approach would work on

The 'Now the world is yours' campaign was aimed at establishing British Airways' name and its new livery in the minds of the public. This was the launch phase, to be followed two weeks later by a shift of emphasis to target selling the new airline to specific categories of customers. The new name was easy enough to remember and so was the new livery. Designed by Negus & Negus, the most striking feature was the aircraft tailfin with a bright-red top and quarter Union Flag – the idea being that in both name and livery there could be no doubt that this was the national airline of Great Britain and stood for the best of British tradition. The quarter Union Flag was a strong enough emblem in itself, lifted with only minor modification from the tailfin emblem of BEA. The white-and-blue fuselage was also strongly reminiscent of BOAC's old livery, all in all a graphic representation of the claim to be 'the best of BEA and BOAC'. With over 220 aircraft flying to over 200 cities in the world in nearly 90 countries, the new British Airways look would soon be one of the most widely seen liveries in the world. For the first time, British Airways was starting to be referred to internally as a 'brand' name. It was nowhere near a masterbrand – that would take some years to secure – but it was rapidly to become associated with a range of product and service brands that would set the industry standards for years to come.

long-haul routes that took seven or more flying hours rather than two or three was questionable to say the least. It would take some ingenuity to devise a successful mixing of essentially different market products on the same aircraft and make it pay.

Despite British Airways' high-cost structure limiting its options, this market opportunity could not be ignored. The yields would be lower and some careful calculations would be needed to make it profitable, but market pricing was an area that British Airways was beginning to understand a great deal better, following the introduction of more modern management thinking into its customer and market research. Understanding what customers really wanted, rather than what the airline thought they would accept, meant that competitive products and services could be developed that customers would appreciate as representing excellent value for money, and these customers would consequently return time and time again.

The problem was that while management were beginning to better understand the theory, the real world was moving on and increasing airline competition forced the introduction of prices and products that, in the long term, were just unsustainable. Advance booking charters (ABCs) offered by the low-cost charter and non-IATA airlines, particularly on the North Atlantic routes, became a significant threat. The late 1970s was a time when price was the prime arbiter in probably the majority of economy travel decisions. The travelling public had never had it so good compared to the higher fares of earlier years. Even standby fares were introduced and, like in the January sales, queues formed outside airline offices overnight to get the best deals. These were the days before computer pricing algorithms could calculate how best to price seats in advance and how many to offer at those low prices. It was a hectic, last-minute, 'first come, first served' approach to allocating seats and checking in the lucky campers, almost the scenario Roy Watts had predicted. Standby-fare customers were almost purely price-driven. What airline they flew on largely did not matter, as long as they arrived safely at their destination. The level of service offered could be, and often was, basic to say the least. The customer promise, if it existed at all, was to take it as you would find it or not at all, a promise that found a resonance in the later 1990s with the rise of the European short-haul, low-cost airlines.

British Airways knew it had to find a way to stand out whatever the market situation. While price clearly mattered, it was only one component in a mix of choices designed to meet differing customers' requirements. It was all about developing the right mix, for the customer and for the business. British Airways certainly had experience from those millions of journeys, and was starting to design the right products and services to meet the demand. There was still a long way to go to control costs, but the company was beginning to realise that, overall, it could be better than the rest – in other words, better by design.

fly BEA to the happiest holiday of all

AND IN MANY CASES

Cheaper than ever before

GET THE BEA BOOK NOW

Advertising on I.T.V.

THE initial venture by the Corporation into the field of commercial television advertising was seen in the North of England on 1st June with the A.B.C. television programme "Holiday Town."

The programme centres around three holiday contests, the first for a television fashion queen, the second for a television bathing beauty, and the third for a television Adonis. The programme visits 13 holiday towns on the north-west and north-east coasts for three months and the winners will be chosen at a grand finale in Blackpool at the beginning of September. They will receive a two weeks' holiday in Bermuda, with air travel in each direction by B.O.A.C. Stratocruiser.

The B.O.A.C. advertisements in the programme appear on four occasions throughout each 45-minute programme, and consist of prominent visual and verbal mentions of the Bermuda service.

The Sales Branch is arranging tie-in displays in each of the towns visited by the programme.

Above: The 'Now the world is yours' launch was at the time the greatest ever advertising campaign by a British travel organisation in the UK, with ninety television spots, five national newspaper colour ads and ninety-four billboard locations over a two-week period – quite low-key coverage by twenty-first-century standards, but considerably more than BOAC's first ever TV advert on 1 June 1957. Launched in the north of England in conjunction with ABC Television's *Holiday Town* programme, the prize for the contestants was a two-week holiday in Bermuda courtesy of BOAC, whose adverts were shown during the programme.

Left: BEA had beaten BOAC to its first TV advert – theirs was launched in in February 1957. Product advertising on TV had only begun two years earlier and BEA's holiday advert was particularly successful. Holiday ads in the 1950s often showed female sun seekers having a jolly time, and the 1957 promotion was no exception. BEA had taken a decision to concentrate its advertising 'on the lower middle and upper working groups, instead of business men and wealthy people', mainly because they represented far more prospective customers, particularly those going on holiday. This decision was with some foresight, as the UK was becoming more prosperous with increasing disposable incomes available for the luxury of an overseas holiday. The UK's improving economy caused the then British Prime Minister, Harold Macmillan, in July 1957, to tell the public they had never had it so good – 'Around the country … you will see a state of prosperity such as we have never had.'

New Poundstretchers from British Airways.
For full details of all Poundstretchers
and conditions of travel, ask at:

Poundstretchers
World-wide low fares 1974/5

Poundstretchers
World-wide low fares 1974/5

British airways

Second edition

British airways

'Poundstretcher low fares' to the Caribbean from £113 return.

British airways
We'll take more care of you.

Fare from London, subject to change and Government approval.

'Poundstretcher low fares' to the South of France from £59 return.

Fare from London, subject to change.

British airways
We'll take more care of you.

Previous page and this spread: On 5 October 1973, British Airways launched the next phase of its publicity campaign by targeting specific categories of customers. The previously wide range of different low fares offered by BEA and BOAC were withdrawn and brought together under a new British Airways 'Poundstretcher' brand. The idea behind the 'Poundstretcher' advertising was 'the fulfilment of an impossible dream, the dream of visiting far-away places, of seeing the sights, of visiting distant friends and relatives, of discovering a new and different way of life'. The opportunities to do all these things were certainly there, as almost every British Airways destination offered a 'Poundstretcher'. For many destinations it was their first real low-fare offering and the brand certainly supported the theme of the British Airways' launch campaign, 'Now the world is yours'. (Foote, Cone & Belding, now DraftFCB London Ltd)

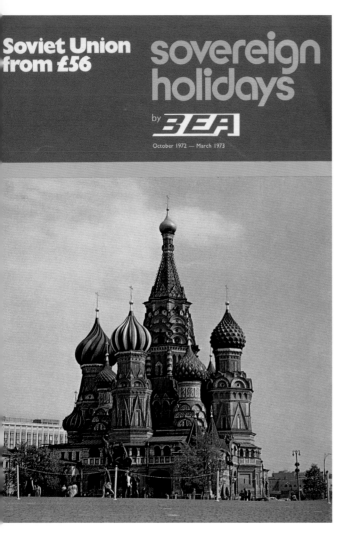

Concurrent with the 'Poundstretcher' launch, British Airways refocussed its inclusive tour brands to take on the well-respected BEA product 'Sovereign Holidays'. Described as 'for discriminating, discerning people who don't like the idea of package holidays', such customers flew on normal scheduled, not charter, services, and flocked in. Business was way above target after the first year, proving the latent demand for a high-end, packaged product.

Right: 'Enterprise' holidays were for the short-haul European market, 'for clients who really want to make every hard-earned penny work for them. So quality at a price most people can afford.' 'Enterprise' holidays were at cut prices that British Airways could afford to offer using the older, inherited aircraft in its fleet such as the 707. Unsurprisingly, so popular were the tours at prices such as Lloret de Mar at £34 for a week, half-board, that business doubled over expectations after the first year.

Far right: BEA had started fly-drive holidays in the 1960s and there was a growing demand for this type of specialised offer. Using scheduled British Airways flights and linking up with the strength of the Avis car hire brand both in Europe and the USA, the 'Freewheeler' fly-drive package introduced in 1974 became a very popular and successful holiday brand product.

This spread: In June 1975 British Airways launched its second major advertising campaign. Called 'Fly the Flag', the purpose was to bring together all previous brand advertising, such as 'Poundstretcher', under one central theme and identity. It was just over one year since the launch of the new airline and it was believed it had built up its image and identity across the world and could now stand alone without any reference back to its predecessor airlines BOAC and BEA. British Airways' new product brands were also becoming well known, and the Union Flag was itself a source of national pride, which the public could identify with the company. 'Fly the Flag' and the associated 'Superflight' advertising campaign saw the beginning of the evolution of British Airways into a masterbrand, although no one called it that at the time, nor thought of it in that way. The use of the term 'brand' across product types was becoming an accepted commonplace term, but it would be at least another decade before 'British Airways' became the leading brand among its range of product brands. In effect, the masterbrand, the one brand to lead them all. (Foote, Cone & Belding, now DraftFCB London Ltd)

British airways

PRAGUE

BUDAPEST

Up to 23 flights weekly to
Eastern Europe

Here's
Superflight.

BOAC

new terminal New York

built for speed

Poundstretchers to Australia from £425 return.

Fly the Flag. British airways

Above: While flying the flag and promoting the brand, British Airways kept up its 'Taking more care of you' message throughout the 1970s and early '80s. 'Care' was considered a strategic message that passengers responded to well. Coupled with a warm and friendly approach, it was a message that broke down the barriers of perceived British reserve. The UK actor Robert Morley, whose warm voice and expansive personality were seen in the all-important US market as epitomising the quintessential Englishman, was seen as almost 'Mr British Airways'. Roz Hanby, a British Airways stewardess and its personality girl, was the front person for the rest of the world, personifying the warm, friendly, total travel experience British Airways promised its passengers.

Left and below: 'Taking more care of you' had to be more than a slogan, however, and needed to be backed up with a real organisation behind the scenes. In 1976 all customer service activities were integrated into a new department, with one of the first actions being to develop superior ground facilities for first-class passengers, particularly at check-in, and, for the first time, the provision of airport lounges at London Heathrow. BOAC had been ahead in lounge development, having introduced a first-class 'Monarch' lounge in 1970 when it opened its new terminal building at New York's John F. Kennedy airport. More would follow around the world in subsequent years as lounges for first- and business-class passengers became a brand expectation rather than a luxury.

TRANSIT LOUNGE

A PASSENGER LOUNGE

This page and next: If one aircraft epitomised the 1970s, it was the 747, introduced on long-haul routes. BOAC considered the aircraft the 'newest and most exciting jetliner of the age'. BOAC was good at this sort of advertising approach. A few years earlier it had made a great play about the travel experience on its VC10 aircraft – 'Supercomfortable, superpowered ... the finest airliner in the world.' What was truly exciting about the 747, however, was its sheer size. It was truly the 'next generation' of aircraft in many ways, but size was the predominant factor. BOAC advertised it as 'more sitting room in the sky' and it raised the bar considerably in terms of passenger space, comfort and overall travel experience. There was just more room to move about, a major improvement on previous long-haul aircraft. The 747 allowed five cabins to be used, each of double width with two aisles, and there was even an upper-deck first-class lounge, the 'club-in-the-sky', as it was called. BOAC even resurrected its old 'Monarch' brand name for the lounge.

✈ BOAC
747

more sitting room in the sky

one flight up
to the Monarch lounge...
an intimate first class club

IT'S JUST A FEW STEPS up the elegant spiral staircase to the BOAC 747 'club-in-the-sky'. In this exclusive-to-first class special compartment is a delightful lounge-bar, furnished with high wide-wing club-style lounge chairs.

Cocktails . . . delicious snacks . . . lively conversation . . . they are all part of flying first class aboard the BOAC 747.

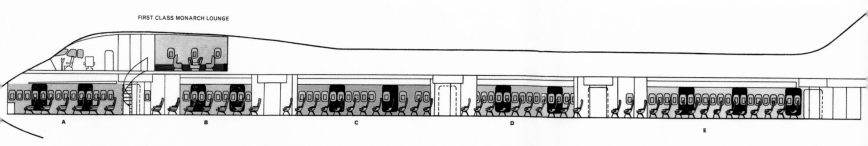

FIRST CLASS MONARCH LOUNGE

A   B   C   D   E

To give its designers maximum scope, BOAC ordered its fleet of 747s unfurnished. The brief to the design team was simple: 'This is a new concept, a revolutionary development, use it to give the customers – all of them – the most spacious comfort in the history of aviation.' Everything was rethought, redesigned, replanned to create that 'sitting room in the sky', the sort of 'spacious comfort' that lived up to BOAC's promise to 'Take good care of you'. To give that almost 'at home' impression, the aircraft bulkheads were hung with real contemporary art, and British Airways continued that feature. In its other new large aircraft – the TriStar-1 – the airline displayed a series of cartoons of imaginary 'machines' by the English artist Rowland Emett. (Right: Rowland Emett)

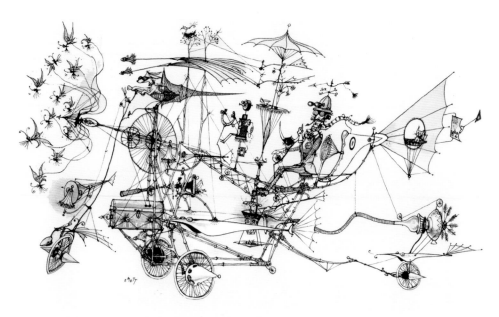

The Featherstone Kite Openwork Basket-Weave Mk. II Gentleman's Flying Machine by Rowland Emett

As featured in the interior decor of the British Airways TriStar Fleet.

Left: Advertisers now had a lot more scope to describe the pleasures of flying in the 747. 'Living space' became a commonly used expression and design creativity would be further stretched in the later 1970s and 1980s as new concepts to cater for new demands would be introduced, not least the introduction of the 'Club Class' cabin in 1978 by British Airways. 'Club' was a name to conjure with, and its association with business and successful people was a deliberate choice. The 747 allowed a separate cabin to be put aside for passengers paying the full economy fare, often people travelling on business who valued the flexibility that a full-fare ticket provided to change flights or cancel at short notice without charge. An experiment in 1977 called the 'Executive' cabin had proven the concept and latent demand, and the 'Club Class' brand was a natural follow-on, firstly on UK–US routes and then worldwide.

Right: It was not all plain sailing, however. Due to the need to cater for fluctuating numbers of business and leisure passengers, the Club cabin often had to be rejigged to increase or reduce it in size using flexible curtain dividers. Not the most attractive way of presenting any cabin, let alone a dedicated business one, but these were early days as all airlines had to learn how best to deal with three distinct levels of on-board customer service on the same long-haul aircraft. The Club Class brand would see several changes over the next decade before the brand promise to deliver could consistently be met worldwide.

Start work in America in less than four hours.

Concorde. From May 29th. London to Washington.

British airways
We'll take more care of you

This page and next spread: Concorde was the product brand that stood above the rest. From its first service to Bahrain in January 1976, Concorde led the British Airways fleet of aircraft for the next twenty-three years. It was a service unique to British Airways and Air France and certainly made the two airlines stand out from the crowd, setting a level of sophistication no other airline could hope to meet. Concorde was at once a great leap forward in technology and a step back in time – many were surprised at how narrow the aircraft cabin was and how small the windows were, although this was more than compensated for by the halving of journey times while enjoying gourmet meals and superior cabin service. Concorde was a brand on a par with the best in the world.

Fly the future – fly the flag with Concorde.

British airways
We'll take more care of you.

Who cares enough to make the world half as big by flying twice as fast?

British airways

British airways **Concorde**

M 2.00

North America from only £75 return.

Now you can fly to New York from £75, and Toronto from £82 by advanced booking charter from London or Glasgow—and with full British Airways service all the way! Now all you need to do is book two months in advance, for full information contact the Overseas Air Travel desk at your nearest British Airways Sales Shop, or your local Travel agent.

(Fuel surcharges as at 1 July 1974 included)

Fares are subject to change

Fly there by OAT British airways

At the other end of the product spectrum, advance booking charters (ABCs) were an attempt by the UK government to introduce simpler, less easily abused charter fares. They effectively destroyed the traditional 'affinity' charter market, as even the scheduled airlines could operate ABCs provided they sold them through a tour operator. Many did, including British Airways through its tour operator Overseas Air Travel, but with a further fall in scheduled prices there was just no need to fly on charters and as the charter market dried up the scheduled service market expanded. Several charter airlines either went bankrupt or converted to become scheduled airlines. Competition was here to stay, and would expand again in the 1980s, which heralded an upturn in fortunes for the aviation market as world economies began to grow.

North America from only £109 return.

Now your clients can experience the super comfort of British Airways service to the USA and Canada from £109 return. OAT flies to New York, Los Angeles and Toronto.

Simply book them with OAT 63 days in advance and they can fly the at charter prices with full British Airways service all the way.

British airways
We'll take more care of you.

OAT ATOL. 038 ABC. Fares from London and subject to change.

3

A NEW IMAGE FOR THE '80S

By the early 1980s British Airways had established its own identity, and BOAC and BEA were just a proud memory. The company had become a well-known and recognised airline across the world. Customers certainly associated the airline with its product brands, such as 'Crown First Class' and 'Super Club', which were becoming increasingly representative of the British Airways overall brand promise. 'Taking more care of you' was becoming a reality, although customer service had still to achieve that step in progress that had been anticipated in the late 1970s. The introduction of Concorde services in 1976 had itself provided a new brand opportunity, a brand that became associated with the highest level of customer service, style and success, a very special service unique to British Airways and Air France.

The 1980s stood out as a decade of change for British Airways. Rising from a financial nadir in 1981/82, when it recorded its largest ever loss as it shook itself free from the cost burden of its predecessor companies, it eventually became known as 'Britain's highest flying company' as it went through a very successful privatisation in January 1987. The 1980s was a decade to remember.

What kick-started that change was a publicity campaign intended to show the world that British Airways was different and better than its competitors. A new public image was particularly important in order to 'puff up' the airline and encourage the public to forget the financial losses and concentrate on the 'new' British Airways, an airline that was different and going places.

'Manhattan is landing ...' was the first of four TV commercials designed by British Airways' new advertising agency, Saatchi & Saatchi, as part of a campaign to place themselves firmly in the public's mind as 'the World's Favourite Airline'. Launched on 10 April 1983, the campaign was very different from anything that had been done before. At that time it was one of the few totally worldwide brand advertising events and was believed to be the most coordinated, broad-scale, international marketing push ever by a British company. It certainly was different, and an image in this book cannot do it justice. Fortunately, it can still be seen in motion on the internet, just as we all saw and were amazed by it all those years ago, before the advent of computer-generated images.

What the campaign made was one big statement, spelled out by Jim Harris, British Airways' Head of Sales. 'We are the world's favourite airline. People of discernment fly with us, people who don't are disappointed.' The campaign did not feature any products, up to then a traditional feature of any airline's ads, but used international celebrities checking in with a British Airways ticket. The ticket brought with it a quiet, cool confidence that came from knowing that most people around the world – especially successful, glamorous people – always make the right choice. Conversely, other 'personalities' were also shown clearly demonstrating their disappointment that they were not flying with British Airways, definitely part of the 'out crowd'.

The campaign focussed on the real difference in flying British Airways, and the fact that more and more people across the world were doing it.

In summer 1980 British Airways introduced reclining 'Sleeperseats' in first class on its 747 services to the US west coast, the Far East, Australia and Africa. First class was also rebranded on those routes to be called 'Crown First Class', both the new seats and the new name an attempt to make the airline stand out as something special and representing 'the highest standards of British Airways' service'. Competition for premium traffic was becoming increasingly tough and the company had to take a lead if it was to break out of its cycle of poor profitability and low productivity. Sleeperseats were promoted as the answer to the problem of sleepless flights on very long sectors, and would eventually become the expected standard for all first-class travel and, subsequently, business travel too.

Saatchi & Saatchi's research had shown that British Airways flew more people to more countries than any other airline, an impressive statistic emphasised by the fact that on the highly competitive North Atlantic routes British Airways carried more people each year than the entire population of Manhattan.

The strapline 'the World's Favourite Airline' and the overall impact of its advertising campaign did hit home to many prospective customers and questioned the traditional presumption that all big airlines are the same. Maybe there really was a difference in flying British Airways, and the overall experience was worth trying. Many did, and it helped lift the company out of the economic downturn of the early 1980s and turn British Airways into 'Britain's highest flying company'. This clearly demonstrated the power of advertising as a promotional medium beamed directly into people's homes via their television sets; the internet, social media and mobile phones had yet to come. Traditional promotional activity still centred on the daily media, roadside billboards, the cinema, radio, the airline's own town offices and travel agents. Capturing the public imagination was the first step towards encouraging them to experience the difference in flying with British Airways.

The 'Manhattan' advertising campaign and the identification of British Airways as 'the World's Favourite Airline' had been only the first step in building a new company. The renewed promise to perform had raised customers' expectations, and these expectations had to be met. The process of improving customer service had been initiated with a 'Putting the Customer First' campaign, which was proving very successful. Customers were beginning to see British Airways in a new and promising light. What was needed now was to bring it all together in a new look, i.e. a new livery. This was considered essential if the travelling public were to believe that British Airways really was better than its competitors and meant business. In fact, the new livery, by the US design house Landor Associates, was very businesslike. Headlined as 'the blue chip style to impress all the world', it

Providing a seat that reclined sufficiently to encourage sleep had been a problem for decades, given the limited space of earlier aircraft. BOAC's Boeing Stratocruiser aircraft had been configured to provide fold-down bunks and recliners in the early 1950s, but it would be nearly another forty years before British Airways took an industry lead with a fully flat bed. BOAC offered 'Slumberette' seats to its first-class 'Majestic' passengers, comfortable by the standards of the day but not much better than a twenty-first-century premium economy seat. (Laban)

This spread: British Airways' business-class Club brand was extended in March 1981 by introducing 'Super Club' on UK–US routes, with the Club brand being retained for the rest of the world. These routes were the most important for premium traffic and invariably launched new and enhanced products. Super Club was quite different from Club in that it offered a new, six-abreast configuration and new 'Expanda' seat, with twenty-four inches between armrests and increased legroom, seat dimensions larger than the old first-class seats. Promoted as 'the widest seat in the business class cabin of any international airline', it set the standard others had to follow if they were to be competitive. In 1984 Super Club was extended to all long-haul routes worldwide.

was indeed corporate and had a clear eye on the anticipated privatisation of British Airways, expected for later in the decade. That could only be achieved if the company became sufficiently profitable over a period of several years to convince investors, particularly corporate investors, the shares were worth holding.

Using Landor Associates was itself a statement of intent to succeed. Landor had grown into the world's largest and most successful design house, with major clients across the globe. Their philosophy was that corporate design was not just a purely creative process and that 'the size, scope and complexities of modern businesses demand that, to be effective, strategic design must literally translate a company's marketing plan into visual form'. In British Airways' case, the design had to reflect 'its professionalism and precision' and be 'simple, distinctive and dignified and demonstrate the airline's commitment to total change that communicates across all customer contact points'. That meant a new image that was British, distinctive and that clearly set out its customer promise, 'To Fly. To Serve.', the first time the airline's motto, from its original heraldic coat of arms, had ever been corporately used. The coat of arms was itself a badge of honour and the new emphasis on its motto was intended to be an unambiguous brand promise to perform.

A new look and new customer service were complemented by a new uniform. As part of the overall British Airways new look, the Roland Klein fashion house was engaged to design a uniform to reflect the new livery and renewed commitment to customer service (its story follows in Chapter 6). Together, Landor and Klein represented the visual transformation of British Airways. They created a powerful new image for the company that took it through a very profitable 1980s and a soaring privatisation in January 1987. The 1990s would present other challenges. Fashions change and so do perceptions of a changing society. The ability to evolve with the times would be seriously tested in the decade to come.

British Airways' revolutionary new approach to European travel.

Two classes to suit the two you's.

Club The Working Class.

For the you that's on business, we now offer the convenience and preferential service of Club.

When you fly Club to Europe, you travel in the calmer, more business-like environment of the separate Club cabin at the front of the aircraft.

You're looked after by extra cabin staff, and served with either a full meal, or high-quality snacks and complimentary drinks.

You can use the exclusive Club check-in desk, select your seat before you board the aircraft, and be amongst those who are the last on and first off.

And you can alter your bookings as often as you like. So your travel plans can be completely flexible.

Yet Club costs only about 5% more than other airlines' standard Economy fares.

Tourist The Leisure Class.

For the you that's spending your own hard-earned money on a leisure flight, we offer the best travel deal in Europe.

Our no-frills Tourist service is available to every major European destination.

It gives you a wide choice of low fares – each with its own special conditions – including our revolutionary Eurobudget fare.

Food and refreshments are available on most routes.

Our simple new two-class system is designed to provide you with precisely the service you need. One kind for the you that's working. And one for the you that isn't.

Find out more from your Travel Agent or British Airways Shop.

British airways
We'll take more care of you.

Opposite left: European routes also received major product changes in early 1981. In what was advertised as 'a revolutionary new approach to European air travel', the old First Class product was discontinued and in its place a Club service was introduced. First Class on short-haul routes had been increasingly seen as an anachronism long past its time, but there remained a demand from business travellers who wanted a fully flexible fare and a higher level of service. Economy was renamed 'Tourist' and advertised as a 'no-frills' service despite having all the amenities of on-board meals, free baggage allowance, etc. 'No frills' would take on an entirely different meaning twenty years later with the rise of the low-cost airlines whose lead-in prices may have been low but whose add-on prices certainly were not. (Foote, Cone & Belding, now DraftFCB London Ltd)

Opposite right and right: 'Manhattan is landing' was a take on the expression used by commercial pilots and air traffic controllers as they confirmed an aircraft's landing approach. As part of the TV advertisement sequence a brightly lit image of the Manhattan skyscraper skyline is seen coming in to land as surprised onlookers watch. In the days of pre-computer-generated images we all watched amazed at such groundbreaking advertising, which was followed by a voiceover that told us British Airways carried more people each year than the population of Manhattan. (Saatchi & Saatchi)

We've got the best connections in Europe

We'll take you to any one of over ninety places all over Europe – that's many more than you can fly to with any other airline.

And we'll take you there faster, more conveniently and more comfortably than anybody else. That's why we're the experts in Europe . . . its Number One airline.

So when you're in Europe, do as the Europeans do and fly BEA . . .

Number 1 in Europe

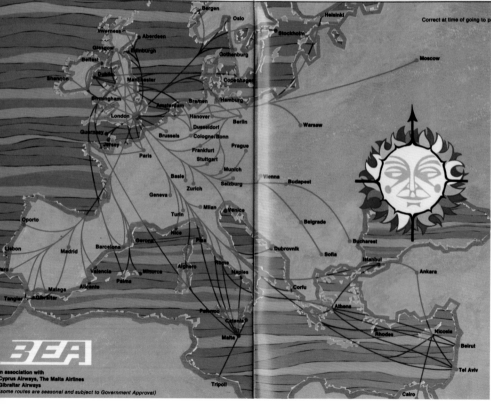

Trident Two
The number 1 way to fly

Number 1 in Europe

This spread: 'Flying more people to more countries' was an advertising story used in the 1960s and early 1970s by BEA and was the basis of BEA's claim to be 'No. 1 in Europe'. The strapline worked well for BEA, so why not British Airways? And so it did, being used extensively and successfully from 1983 for many years in conjunction with the accolade of 'the World's Favourite Airline'. (This page: Saatchi & Saatchi)

Departure.   Arrival.

Our new look arrived December 5th. **BRITISH AIRWAYS**
The world's favourite airline

This spread: British Airways' new image by Landor Associates was a critical part of its strategy to be seen as a global player in the rapidly expanding travel market of the 1980s. The company believed its old image was out of step with its new service-led culture and its 'emphasis on technological capability and electronic-style precision'. A new image was required that would allow it to 'brand the total experience from baggage tags to aircraft, producing a totally unified and integrated system of names, graphic identities, livery design, ground equipment, interiors, sales shops', etc., in other words, apart from retaining the company's name, change everything.

This was a complete and necessary break with the past. The old Negus & Negus livery had done its job to bring together the identities of BOAC and BEA, retain both staff and customer loyalties and be sufficiently bold to make the then new company stand out. It was, however, now considered a bit too linked to the past, a bit 'Carnaby Street' in its 'strident primary colours' of red, white and blue. The focus on its abbreviated name 'British', was also considered 'an overly-aggressive nationalistic statement, which was strongly negative, particularly in some parts of the Commonwealth', but the Union Flag element of the old livery was an important element and needed to be retained. It was indicative of British Airways' position as the national airline of the UK and was something that made it stand out among a growing number of private UK airlines. (Above: Saatchi & Saatchi)

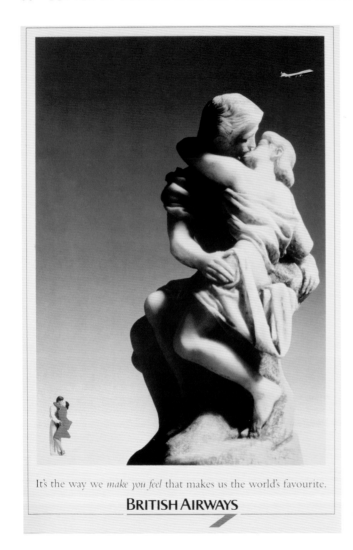

It's the way we *make you feel* that makes us the world's favourite.

BRITISH AIRWAYS

BRITISH AIRWAYS

Far left: The new Landor livery had been tested through market research against the attributes of 'reliable, distinctive, modern, exciting, warm and British' – attributes that would surface time and time again as British Airways evolved over the succeeding decades. Under Landor they were encapsulated by the line 'It's the way we *make you feel* that makes us the world's favourite.' (Saatchi & Saatchi)

Left: The Landor livery design was considered by them to represent '80% of precision and professionalism and 20% on pride of origin'. It certainly looked precise and professional, with a palette of very corporate midnight blue and silver grey with a sweeping and sharp red 'Speedwing' line along the fuselage, an 'evolving' of the old 'Speedbird' logo stretched and repainted into a design for the 1980s. (Saatchi & Saatchi)

BRITISH AIRWAYS COAT OF ARMS

The Landor tailfin design retained the quarter Union Flag but in more muted shades and carried through the midnight blue along its top half to provide a sharp background colour to a contemporary interpretation of the British Airways heraldic coat of arms and its motto 'To Fly. To Serve.', the first time it had ever been promoted as an element of the company's livery. The retention of the flag and dark blue from the Negus & Negus design were also considered core elements to retain in order 'to protect the franchise', the inclusion of the coat of arms a 'hallmark of quality and grace'. It was certainly a quality look, reflecting a new and positive, customer-orientated, corporate British Airways, a new look to go with a new airline aiming for privatisation well before the end of the decade.

G-BOAD

More international travellers choose to fly with British Airways than with any other airline.

Every day, one airline sells more international tickets than any of its competitors.

Last year an average of over 53,000 per day across our scheduled and charter operations.

Tickets taking nearly 20 million people to destinations all around the world.

In fact, on an average day, 575 of our flights take off somewhere on the globe. (That's one flight every three minutes – about the time it takes to read this advertisement.)

If that surprises you, you are probably unaware that since 1973, British Airways has consistently flown more people internationally than any other airline.

We also have the largest fleet of any European airline, with 159 aircraft in operation.

But the most important fact of all is that we have now become one of the most profitable international airlines in the world.

Which all goes to prove that British Airways is no fly-by-night company.

BRITISH AIRWAYS

Britain's highest flying company.

To complete the British Airways new look a new uniform had been designed by the French couturier Roland Klein. That story is set out in Chapter 6 and its 'Flight into Fashion'. The Klein uniform was an integral part of the new look and feel of British Airways and was extensively used in advertising throughout the rest of the 1980s and early 1990s. (Left and below: Saatchi & Saatchi)

Someone up there is looking after you.

No matter where your business takes you, rest assured that British Airways people will smooth the way with superb service and the most convenient connections round the world. It's simply because of our unique training program in the finer points of looking after our passengers . . . among other things.

BRITISH AIRWAYS

The world's favourite airline.

This page and next: Once privatisation was completed in January 1987, British Airways could concentrate on further refining its product brands. In November it announced a new deal for the business passenger, aiming to make the airline 'the best in business'. The core was two new product brands, 'Club World' and 'Club Europe'. On long-haul routes Super Club had been very successful putting British Airways into a competitive lead; Club in Europe had also successfully replaced the old First Class. Competitors were, however, catching up. On long-haul routes the continuing use of a curtain cabin divider was clearly more for the airline's operational needs rather than those of its customers and had to go. In Europe the brand name Club had also lost its exclusivity and needed change. Both these business traveller markets were arguably the most important for the airline, and the lead had to be retaken.

In January 1988 Club World and Club Europe were launched, accompanied by a complete refurbishment of their respective cabin interiors and improved on-board service with dedicated cabin crew and enhanced ground facilities. Significantly for Club World, a 'Slumberseat' and dedicated cabin was also introduced. The new seat gave the business traveller for the first time not a flat bed, but one not far removed from that offered in Crown First Class. This was part of a new approach to the way British Airways would market itself with the new business classes; it was the first of a range of product brands to be launched in a bid to encourage greater customer loyalty and win a bigger slice of the worldwide business travel market.

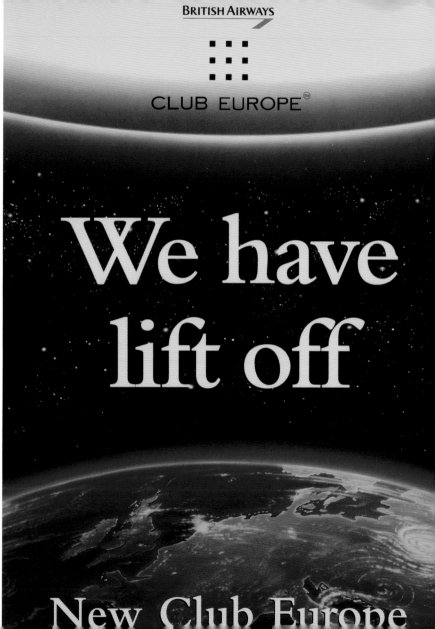

BRITISH AIRWAYS

CLUB EUROPE

We have lift off

New Club Europe

THE ONLY WAY TO ARRIVE IN 1988.

Above: Crown First Class reverted back to 'First Class' and was relaunched with a £24 million investment in product improvements. The new name was hardly a game changer, but together with the Club brands it did represent a gradual coming together of a coherent set of product brand names and services that would set their respective standards for the next decade.

Right: Not to be outdone, Concorde services were also enhanced as part of the Landor 'new look' and, in 1987, its services were extended to Barbados. This route was strongly supported by a wealthy clientele as well as many others who just wanted to fly on the supersonic aircraft, a fabulous way to start (or end) a holiday. One of British Airways' retired fleet of Concordes is now a major tourist attraction at Barbados's Grantley Adams Airport. (Saatchi & Saatchi)

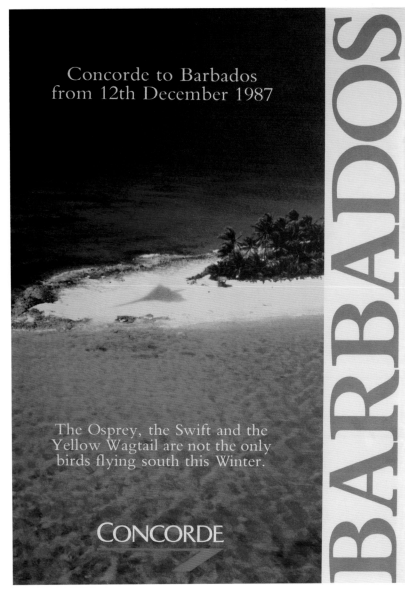

Concorde to Barbados
from 12th December 1987

The Osprey, the Swift and the
Yellow Wagtail are not the only
birds flying south this Winter.

CONCORDE

BARBADOS

Left and below: A brand presence on the high street, either in their own offices or through travel agents, remained an integral part of any airline's sales capabilities well into the late 1990s. To draw in prospective customers, airline shop windows were often used for high-end promotional purposes. In 1963, when London cinemas were screening the European premiere of *Cleopatra*, BOAC loaned several film props and outfits used by the film's leading actress, Elizabeth Taylor, as part of a window display promoting the film and inclusive tours to Egypt. (Left: Adelman)

Opposite: New computing and internet technology would eventually drastically reduce dependency on travel agencies and even the airline's own travel shop, but during the 1980s and 1990s the high street was still where many people bought their airline tickets and made reservations. British Airways' main London travel shops were amalgamated and moved to 156 Regent Street in October 1989. The new and greatly enlarged 'flagship store' was to become the airline's main retail outlet, offering 'excellent service, customer care and travel technology', a one-stop shop for everyone's travel needs including several luxury leisure product retail outlets, a cafe and a travel immunisation clinic.

   Certainly part of the British Airways' brand experience, Regent Street was eventually closed in 2006 as part of a general closure of the British Airways travel shops network. Online bookings and paperless ticketing had effectively undercut the substantial cost of a high-street presence and the closure became yet another part of the changing face of the airline world in the twenty-first century.

TRAVEL MADE EASY

Flying is the simplest way of travelling about the world, but you
will find the specialized knowledge and services of the
Travel Agent invaluable. No amount of travel experience can
replace his expert advice and assistance. Whenever and wherever
you fly, consult your local B.O.A.C. Appointed Agent —
he is there to help you.

B R I T I S H   O V E R S E A S   A I R W A Y S   C O R P O R A T I O N
IN ASSOCIATION WITH QANTAS EMPIRE AIRWAYS LIMITED · SOUTH AFRICAN AIRWAYS AND TASMAN EMPIRE AIRWAYS LIMITED

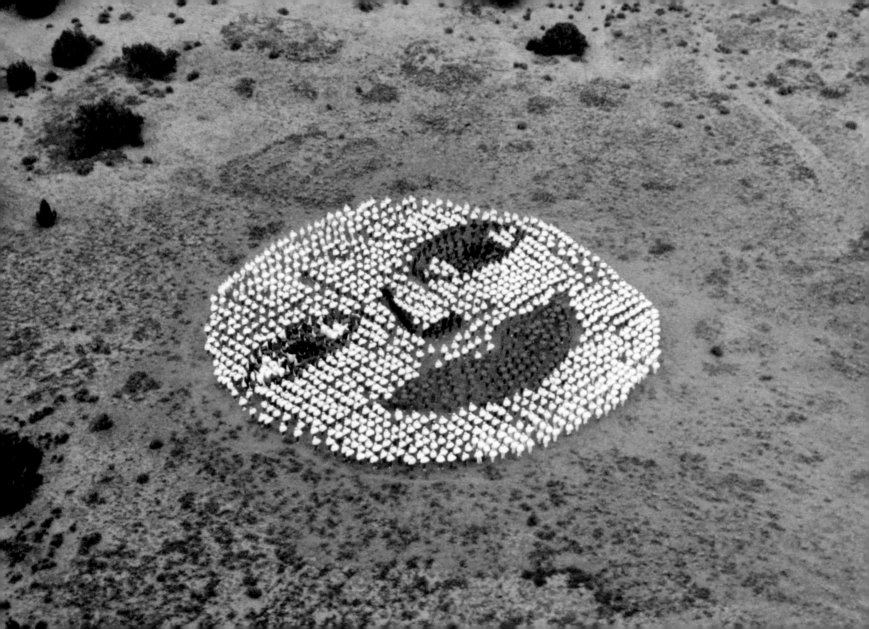

4

GOING GLOBAL IN THE '90S

By the end of the 1980s British Airways had maintained its position as 'the World's Favourite Airline', but had also moved into the position of one of the world's most profitable airlines. The six years since the launch of 'Manhattan is Landing' had seen its profits transform, leading to a very successful privatisation in January 1987, the introduction and refinement of several key products and services, and a reputation for caring, friendly service. In 1988, the British Airways Chairman, Lord King of Wartnaby, set out what he called 'a clear ambition. We want British Airways to be the best and most successful airline in the world,' adding, 'What's wrong with that?' Well, nothing really. Everyone would benefit: customers, shareholders, staff and certainly the UK economy.

Opposite and next page: Designed to achieve as great an impact as the 'Manhattan is Landing' advertising of the early 1980s, a spectacular new global advertising campaign was launched on Christmas Eve 1989, positioning British Airways as the leading global airline of the new decade. Called 'Global', the advert's emphasis was on the airline's 'caring and friendly qualities of its customer service and the size and reach of its international route network'. The ad had a cast of over 4,000 people, most of whom were US high school or university students, performing co-ordinated movements to form friendly faces and global images. Directed by Hugh Hudson, the director of the Oscar-winning film *Chariots of Fire*, it could hardly fail to make an impact.

The 1990s was the decade of airline globalisation; alliances of airlines were beginning to form and would become the dominant feature of the airline world for the foreseeable future. 'Global' set the scene very well and would lead to many more far-reaching changes in British Airways' approach to its overall brand positioning as the decade progressed. (Saatchi & Saatchi)

British Airways was actually very well placed to take advantage of the rapidly falling commercial barriers; it could innovate where it had been restricted before and operate new routes where it saw its best business interests without requiring the traditional permissions. This was very important, especially in Europe, where the European Union countries had at last, and rather reluctantly, agreed to a fairly liberal common air-transport policy that would offer, at least in theory, some new business opportunities. Without this new freedom there was a real risk that air services to and from Europe could become dominated by the US mega-carriers, such as American Airlines and United, who had survived the fallout of US deregulation in the previous decades. These airlines were not only huge with extensive route networks, especially to internal US cities, but they were very experienced, customer-savvy and ahead of the pack in rapidly developing computer technology, technology that would become critical in future years, especially in selling airline seat reservations. Unlike some of its European competitors, many still nationalised and overprotected, British Airways could take this level of new competition. It had faced many years of the cut-and-thrust of competition in its own backyard with, by the late 1980s, at least twelve directly competing UK airlines operating domestic and international services. It was the largest carrier of international airline traffic in the world and had climbed to a leading place in the league table of the world's most profitable airlines. The airline had a better control of its costs than ever before and was now in control of its own destiny, no longer dependent upon the dead

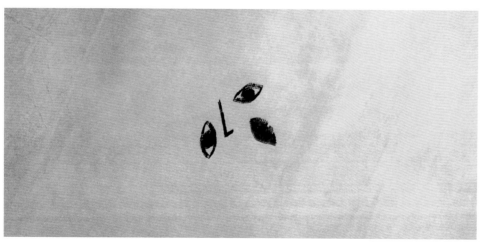

hand of government and UK Treasury limitations. If any company could succeed, then why not British Airways?

It was time for a new worldwide advertising campaign to launch British Airways into the 1990s. Called 'Global', it was another groundbreaking creation by Saatchi & Saatchi that brought together two key values in one proposition – the caring and friendly characteristics of British Airways' people and the sheer size of the airline's network. These two powerful values lay at the heart of the campaign, which launched on 24 December 1989, Christmas Eve – what better time to emphasise that British Airways had achieved its goal to be the best, and that, with the warmth and humanity of its people coupled with its overall professionalism and efficiency, it did stand out from the crowd.

At this point it is worth mulling over a few statistics to put in context this brand promise to be warm and caring, professional and efficient, each and every time. When the 'Global' campaign was launched, a British Airways aircraft was made ready for take-off somewhere around the world every 117 seconds – nearly every two minutes, twenty-four hours a day, every day of the year, including Christmas Day. If it was a 747, some 40,150 items would have been loaded for every flight, and across the airline's fleet of 211 different aircraft, 120,000 meals were prepared each week. These flights carried 24.6 million passengers each year, which breaks down to forty-six passengers checking in somewhere in the world every minute of every day, non-stop. Numbers to conjure with, but whichever way they are cast they are impressive.

The accolade 'the World's Favourite Airline' could thus

be measured in simple numbers, but it was much more than that – to keep this accolade year after year meant that British Airways must have got something right and was delivering on its brand promise to perform time and time again. This also meant there was a clear recognition of the British Airways brand image across the world – in effect it was a masterbrand with associated product brands – but was it strong enough to take the company through another decade, and what did it now represent?

Known as the 'Masterbrand Repositioning Programme', research was initiated in 1993 that looked closely into the perceptions and visual impact of the British Airways image across markets and consumers, with the aim to becoming 'The first choice airline all over the world'. Many saw the company as safe, reliable and professional, very 'British' – all positive attributes, but these were countered by other perceptions that it was too formal, brittle even, and lacking in warmth and 'humanity'. This was a bit of a surprise and not quite what might be expected, given one of the main aims of the 'Global' campaign was to create an image of warmth and humanity to add to the airline's professional and efficient image (although the previous decade's focus on a very corporate and professional style had almost inevitably led it that way). Two very tangible strengths remained, however – the company's global reach and caring image – both strengths that could, it was felt, become the focus for meeting every customer's needs.

British Airways' original promise of 'Taking more care of you' had clearly not got lost along the way, but it needed to be brought out as part of a real and meaningful initiative and not just part of some new marketing campaign. Attending to customers' needs and comforts needed to become a routine rather than the exception; each customer must be treated with warmth and sensitivity and they must be made to feel valued and 'at home'. Making the routine exceptional, however, would need more work than a short-term advertising splash; the principles and practices must be embedded to ensure that this became an enduring and natural expectation of British Airways' overall service and brand promise. This meant beginning to explore the scope of human diversity, looking at people's relationships, feelings and expressions. Such human factors were explored in what became known as 'The People Concept', given visual form in TV and above-the-line media as different people in different (happy) moods with a subtle background of British Airways' global resources. Such a global, caring, people-orientated theme became the bedrock of British Airways' brand promise for the 1990s. It also led the way towards a wider concept and image of the company as more than the world's favourite – it was itself a twenty-first-century world citizen.

BRITISH AIRWAYS

Step into a *new* world.

It's the way we *make business travellers* feel
that makes us the world's favourite.

British Airways started the 1990s as it
meant to go on. 'Step into a *new* world', the
brochure says, with an emphasis on 'It's
the way we *make business travellers* feel
that makes us the world's favourite.' This
was all about promoting the new world for
business customers that it had launched in
the late 1980s: 'Increased service. Greater
comfort. More freedom' in the new Club
World, First Class and Concorde.

A British Airways 747 at Heathrow in the early 1990s with 40,150 essential items that must be packed for each flight: eight tonnes of catering, everything for the care and comfort of 400 passengers to meet their respective expectations each and every day of the year.

Left: Although British Airways was focussing on business customers, it had not forgotten the increasingly important leisure travel market. Hit by world economic uncertainties following the August 1990 invasion of Kuwait, the business market was softening but the leisure travel market was actually buoyant, rising by around 14 per cent. British Airways had recognised for some time that cost pressures, particularly fuel costs, would bear heavily on the industry in future years and the leisure market could not be ignored. It then represented over 50 per cent of the airline's revenue, and new investment in its economy brands needed to be made in order to keep the business secure.

Market research had shown that there was a very diverse range of passenger types travelling in economy, so-called 'empty-nesters', 'energetic families', 'strivers', 'reluctant travellers': an eclectic mix of travellers whose expectations and needs were different but who were, as a group, more likely to react to their travel experience because they were not necessarily regular travellers. For most, the flight itself was part of their holiday experience; in-flight service was therefore seen as an important differentiator between airlines.

Personal service was seen as a key factor and cabin crews were to be given more time serving their passengers than ever before. This was very much about improving the whole customer experience from the moment of welcome at check-in to saying goodbye at the final destination. Launched in November 1990, the economy travel experience on British Airways was given a major upgrade and two new brand names: 'World Traveller' for long haul and 'Euro Traveller' for short haul, from new cabin colour schemes to improved meal quality and choice and everything in between. This was not just a rebranding exercise but a major move away from the perception of some that economy passengers were second-class citizens travelling 'down the back'. They were valued customers, to be treated with full attention and respect with a high-quality service and product no matter what they had paid or where they were seated on the aircraft. This was very much about being seen as 'warm and friendly'; the attributes the 'Global' campaign had impressed us with really was the new British Airways.

Next three pages: 'Feeling good' was the theme for a range of advertising posters preceding the masterbrand repositioning. Destination ads along the theme of happy people and exotic places were also issued. They certainly represented the latest genre of very good graphic and photographic images, the sort of images people would want to put on a wall, a constant reminder of their travel experience with British Airways, and many did. (Saatchi & Saatchi)

It's the way we *make you feel* that makes us the world's favourite.

BRITISH AIRWAYS

It's the way we *make you feel* that makes us the world's favourite.

BRITISH AIRWAYS

It's the way we *make you feel* that makes us the world's favourite.

BRITISH AIRWAYS

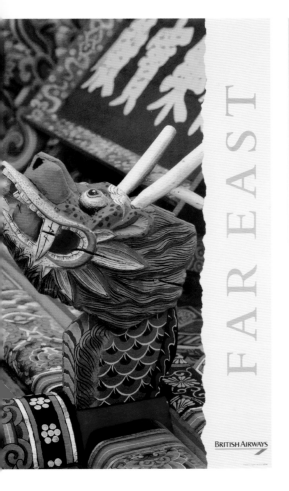

ENGLAND

BRITISH AIRWAYS

ITALY

BRITISH AIRWAYS

THERE ARE
MORE THINGS
THAT BRING
US TOGETHER
THAN KEEP US
APART.

Shonali Bulchandani
Bride
Bombay
India

Christina Allert
Bride
Greve
Denmark

This spread: 'There are more things that keep us together than keep us apart' was a strapline used as part of the masterbrand repositioning. This was a clever play on human emotions. In the advert emotions are shown as common to any bride across the world; emotions span the breadth of human diversity and cultures, a shared humanity that links people together. This was all about embedding the global and caring side of British Airways in the minds of prospective customers; it was a softer, simpler, more emotionally focussed style of advertising to demonstrate the airline was uniquely positioned to understand all its customers around the world and its role in bringing people together. (Opposite: Saatchi & Saatchi)

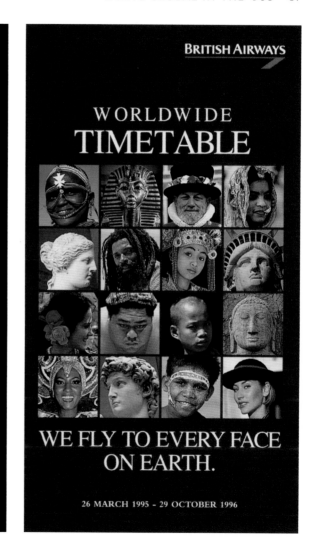

Take a seat and enjoy more living room

A new angle on comfort.
With its unique tilting action and ergonomic 'cradle' design, our new seat fully supports your body throughout your flight.

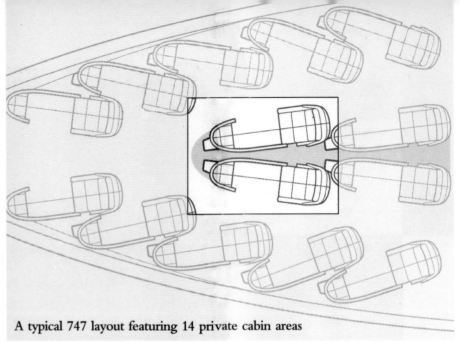

A typical 747 layout featuring 14 private cabin areas

This spread: The masterbrand repositioning was accompanied by another major campaign called 'Insight' that launched in September 1995 – a £500 million, three-year plan to improve every aspect of customer service. British Airways was certainly not short of initiatives in the 1990s and was taking its focus on customer service to yet new territory: starting with First Class, the product was renamed 'First', and meant it; it introduced the world's first ever fully flat full-length bed on an airline.

Maintaining and enhancing the First product was a deliberate choice to differentiate clearly between First and Club World as two distinct premium products to give customers the best choice and range of travel options. Club World was also improved, with a new 'cradle' seat with improved legroom and recline, not quite a bed, but nearly. That would come not much later. Club Europe was also enhanced with its own new and wider seat, to be followed in November 1998 with another £150 million investment in the World Traveller product and further Club Europe improvements less than a year after that. British Airways was spending an eye-watering amount of money to keep its brand promise to all its passengers no matter what they paid or where they sat. This was a brand promise with real meaning that would stand it in good stead in the rapidly approaching twenty-first century, when the meaning of being a 'full service' airline would be severely tested, but British Airways would not be found wanting.

World Traveller - the world of difference to leisure travel

CLUB EUROPE
BRITISH AIRWAYS

More flights, more frequently, to more European destinations, than any other airline.

- 70 destinations across Europe, with just under 500 departures each day
- New, contemporary menus with fresher and healthier meals from all over Europe
- A generous hand baggage allowance of 18kg (two pieces of 9kg each)
- The choice of 10 different check-in options – including self-service machines allowing check-in in under a minute
- Access to 26 lounges across Europe

What also stood out in the 1990s was the rapid change in opportunities for direct airline-to-customer contact driven by advances in technology and the need to control costs. Call centre development that had really begun to take off in the previous decade was refined and improved and started to provide the basis for performance management and overall efficiencies; it was a real alternative to using travel agents as going to the airline directly via a call centre or online could save money for customers through lower direct fare offers.

'World Offers' had been used as a promotional slogan since the early 1990s when it was first used to kick-start a slow market following the first Gulf War and was regularly used in later years as a strategic umbrella campaign for low-fare messages. A British Airways Regent Street office staff member hands out World Offers leaflets to passing shoppers in early 1999 during another slow market. Temptingly low prices and very big shop-window adverts were a proven draw everywhere, as in Poland, where queues formed on 23 January 1999 to buy tickets at half price.

5

BECOMING A TWENTY-FIRST-CENTURY WORLD CITIZEN

By the end of the 1990s the sheer scale of British Airways' operations had led many people to see the company as a leader among airlines. Being big, reliable and prestigious were not, however, considered within British Airways to be the key ingredients for the twenty-first century. The late 1990s masterbrand repositioning study had refocussed the airline's advertising to become more people-orientated with a strong humanitarian element, but it was only the first step towards embracing still softer values. While the 1980s big-business values had produced a very successful company, being seen as more global, approachable and cosmopolitan was the new way to go.

British Airways had evolved into a clearly recognisable international brand and a product brand leader possessing considerable 'image' capital, expressed as 'a mixture of recollection, association and expectation shared by all successful businesses'. The big issue was the belief that to be a truly global brand the company needed more than just a common identity, i.e. the masterbrand element. While the Landor livery had placed British Airways on the world brand stage and had done its job well, what was now needed was a recognisable symbol of an organisation attuned to a rapidly shrinking world with a melee of different cultures, interests and a much looser affiliation to national identity. The new approach was to be 'global and caring' with a multinational identity representative of a world airline in the twenty-first century.

On 10 June 1997 British Airways unveiled a new corporate image and mission: 'To be the undisputed leader in world travel.' It was one of the most massive rebranding exercises in corporate history. The company's entire fleet of aircraft, vehicles, stationery, catering, the uniforms of its customer contact staff, in fact everything that moved and (almost) everything that did not move, received a dynamic new look. It was much more than a change of graphics – it was intended also as a change in culture to reflect and incorporate that global and caring approach, the latter a much more difficult trick to achieve than with simply a lick of new paint. This new philosophy would build on British Airways' undisputed reputation for customer service and take it into a 'more globally minded future'. If it was to succeed it would be particularly important to redirect the airline's internal culture; new management and customer service training programmes were introduced with the ambitious target to become the 'best-managed company in Europe and the world by 2000'. If the key to success is to appreciate that you soon become what you intend to be, then it was a fine ambition to go for.

The essence of the new image was to turn around the perception of British Airways as a British airline with global operations and morph it overnight 'to become a world airline whose headquarters happen to be in Britain', that is to say a world brand and not just a worldwide brand.

Turning its fleet into a flying art gallery was one way to gain instant attention, although some said it did not make British Airways stand out from the crowd as its many tailfin designs became lost in the plethora of airline liveries at busy airports. The nearly fifty different designs were without question bold and innovative, and were a fine tribute to the imagination and skill of many artists and craftsmen and women from around the world. Chris Holt, British Airways Head of Design Management, summed up the philosophy behind the change: 'The richness, colour and diversity that these images represent capture the company's commitment to adopt a more cosmopolitan approach in the years ahead.' With the benefit of hindsight, the philosophy and commitment could not be faulted. What was misunderstood was the UK public's likely reaction: tradition and not transformation was the expectation of the UK's national airline.

This subtle redefinition would literally see the airline in very new colours. In fact, very many new colours, explained in the launch publicity as 'a creative expression of a company which, both in the letter and the spirit, regards the whole world as its customer' and that 'global and caring' does not mean post-imperialist flag-waving. It has to mean intelligently sensitive relations with customers and communities. Some thought that was what British Airways had always tried to do – within the limitations of international airline business, it had always been respectful and understanding of different cultures and traditions. A new livery was not going to change that, nor was an attempt to impose a culture of informality as a means by which to emphasise a new style of 'caring'. Customer surveys had shown that cabin crews should retain their professionalism but be more informal, a little less 'British'. In future, cabin crew were to be taught how to 'study their passengers and adapt their personalities to suit the clientele'; that's all very well, but forcing a personality change risks being seen as transparent and not truly 'caring', being 'British' one minute and not 'British' the next – a conjuring trick with risks and difficult for any but the best to perform.

British Airways' new cabin crew training programme was called 'Kaleidoscope', a very apt title for a programme linked to the introduction of the airline's new livery, itself a kaleidoscope of colour and patterns from around the world. These new colours were certainly that 'creative expression', turning what was previously a uniform identity into one of variety that reflected global interests. Using the works of artists and craftsmen from around the world, British Airways' fleet of aircraft was to be the most visible expression of the new company. What became known as the 'World Images' livery was intended to be reflective of different cultures and communities, but was meant to be much more than artistic paintwork. It was meant to indicate an appreciation of different people's views, needs and expectations, recognising and respecting differences, above all understanding people and reflecting that in the service offered.

If British Airways could achieve all that, it would put the airline into a different league.

'World Images' was a very new and rather refreshing philosophy. Devised under the optimistic title of 'Project Utopia', it was another good example of British Airways pushing the envelope into uncharted waters, the sort of thing leading companies do, constantly challenging accepted custom and practice. It is that sort of process that makes for great companies, but changes of this sort of magnitude also include great risks. With 60 per cent of British Airways' business originating from overseas, the risks appeared low. Such a business should have little loyalty to the concept of 'Britishness' but should embrace the concept of the airline as a 'world citizen', and many people did. Unfortunately, a large and vocal slice of the remaining, UK-originating 40 per cent took the other view. The rather fine point of British Airways 'becoming a world airline that just happened to have its headquarters in Britain' was, disappointingly, lost, and the public and media's perception ranged from welcoming through perplexed curiosity to instant dislike. British Airways was still perceived by probably the majority of British travellers as the British national airline – it may have been 'the World's Favourite Airline', but it was British born and based, and not some chameleon-like concept of multi-nationality.

The 'World Images' kaleidoscope of colours did not last. From 1999, in recognition that a more balanced reflection of British heritage was also required, around half of British Airways' aircraft were repainted in the 'World Image' that was designed for Concorde – ironically a simple, graphic design of the Union Flag known as the Chatham Flag design. The flagship's uncompromisingly British standard was thus passed to the fleet and, in time, became the central design of the British Airways masterbrand. As a concept, 'World Images' was certainly groundbreaking. The belief and passion behind its 'utopian' ideals were laudable, but for many it was a step too far.

Far left: The traditional rock painting art of the Ncoakhoe tribe of the San people of the Kalahari Desert by the artist Cgoise, one of five women in a group of tribal artists working out of the Kuru Development Trust, an indigenous organisation for the self-development of the San people. This artwork can be seen in British Airways' headquarters building at Harmondsworth, near Heathrow. (Cgoise)

Left: Colour down the Side by the British artist Terry Frost. This painting can be seen in the British Airways arrivals lounge in Heathrow Terminal 5. (Terry Frost)

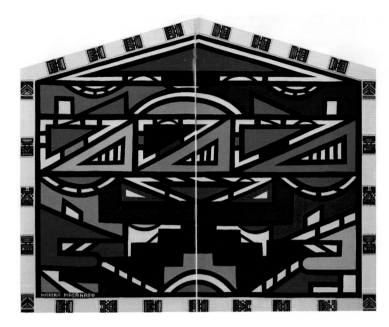

Above: The bold, abstract patterns created by the Ndebele people of the Transvaal, South Africa, have earned them the title of 'the artist nation', and their work is known and respected worldwide. The twin sisters Emmly and Martha Masanabo created this mural-style enamel painting for British Airways bordered with swags of beadwork. (Emmly and Martha Masanabo)

Right: Whale Rider is the title of this image of a painted wood carving by Joe David of the Tla O Qui Aht tribe from western Canada. The carving reflects the symbolism and narrative themes of the tribe's traditional artworks and can be seen in the British Airways headquarters building at Harmondsworth, near Heathrow. (Joe David)

The Historic Dockyard, Chatham, United Kingdom

The Union Flag
Aircraft Type: Concorde

The Union Flag is the official name for the national flag of the United Kingdom. It was first created in 1606 to represent the union of England and Scotland by combining the crosses of St George and St Andrew, and in 1801 - when Ireland was incorporated into Great Britain - the cross of St Patrick was added, creating a simple, graphic design in red, white and blue that is an immediately recognisable symbol of the United Kingdom. This flag was stitched by The Admiral's Original Flag Loft in Chatham's Historic Dockyards, Kent, which has been making high quality flags for more than 400 years.

BRITISH AIRWAYS

Left: A poster explains the history of the Union Flag and its making in Chatham Historic Dockyard. (Chatham Historic Dockyard)

Right: Coupled with the livery launch was a new advertising campaign to tug the heartstrings. Unsurprisingly, it was another blockbuster launch, described as 'the world's largest-ever corporate television broadcast'. TV, cinema, press, posters and radio all featured the campaign, coordinated with simultaneous launches to 126 invited audiences in 63 countries around the world. Under the strapline 'The world is closer than you think', the campaign portrayed British Airways as global and caring and committed to serving all the communities of the world. It again emphasised the sense of shared emotion that travel can bring between diverse communities and the company's role in understanding and enabling the travel experience. (MCSaatchi)

It seems there's this enormous fish that travels the world without getting cau[ght]

The world is closer than you think.

BRITISH AIRWAYS
The world's favourite airline

6

FLIGHT INTO FASHION

'Fashion is not something that exists in dresses only. Fashion is in the sky, in the street, fashion has to do with ideas, the way we live, what is happening.' Coco Chanel may not have been thinking specifically about aviation in the 1950s when she made that statement, but it sums up the reality of the overall pervasiveness of fashion in everything we do. Fashion is everywhere and in everything – it is in what we wear, in how we live and socialise.

Fashion is certainly present across the whole spectrum of aviation, although we tend to think of it more in a technological design sense, always moving forward – plastics replacing wood and Bakelite, jet engines replacing propellers, carbon fibre replacing metal. In aviation, technology rarely moves backwards; it is very unlikely there would ever be a return to biplane aircraft or flying boats. Fashion in what we wear, however, goes back and forth. What may be long this year is short the next, or nipped and tucked like seasons past. Some things don't change. Practicality, durability even, is often essential, not least with airline uniforms. This season's diaphanous creation may look good on a fashion-show runway but it would not be very practical in a galley or while looking after customers. A protective cover-all would better suit some situations, but the best balance is to be found in a blend of practicality and style, ideally with a touch of haute couture.

British Airways' flight into fashion was initiated in the late 1960s, even before its formation. It was the start of a relationship with figures at the top of British haute couture that endured over three successive uniform designs. The 1960s also heralded a change in the perception of and design of female cabin crew uniforms – a term previously unheard of, as female crew on British Airways' predecessor companies, BOAC and BEA, were called stewardesses. In the 1940s BEA called both male and female cabin crew 'stewards', a title that was the epitome of gender equality but applied for a very different reason.

The increasingly affluent teenage population of the 1960s was the catalyst for a profound social change which saw the London fashion schools and fashion houses setting trends that remain with us still. The pace of change rapidly affected the perception of airline staff. They were not just wearing 'uniforms' but clothing that reflected both the spirit of the time and the brand values the airline represented. The fashion trends of the 1960s 'jet set' were not just for high-flying customers but identified with the airline staff themselves. How the staff looked, no longer just in 1950s terms of being 'neat, efficient and cheerful' but also 'of a pleasing appearance', was now much more important.

It is also worth mentioning another catalyst in the explosion of changing women's fashion during that time. In 1960 the UK lifted its embargo on US fashion imports, an embargo imposed years earlier to protect the UK clothing industry. The USA speciality was ready-made, mass-produced clothing using new, man-made materials such as nylon and synthetic and coated cottons. Such 'fast-drying, figure hugging' materials meant low costs and rapid turnarounds in stock and styles, not unlike the twenty-first-century Primark offering. Coupled with the USA's entrepreneurial

TEXTILES FROM BRITAIN

Wings over the World
THE MAGAZINE OF BOAC AUGUST 1946

BOAC's 1946 in-flight magazine was called *Wings over the World*. It was widely used as an advertising platform for the output of British designers and manufacturers and fashion took a prime position in each issue. As the nationalised airlines of the UK, BOAC and BEA were expected to promote British interests, even at a cost to themselves. This 'we are all in it together' approach was very much in the spirit of the time. The 'Textiles from Britain' advert shows a selection of silk scarves from companies such as Jacqmar, Roosen, F. W. Grafton, etc. Jacqmar maintained an association with BOAC and BEA for many years, producing scarves as on-board sale and promotional items and as uniform accessories. (Above: F. H. K. Henrion)

spirit, epitomised by New York's Seventh Avenue fashion-retailing centre, these new materials ensured that 'frou-frou freight' – as it was called by some in BOAC – was on its way.

BEA was the acknowledged No. 1 airline in Europe, and in the mid-1960s it commissioned the UK's then No. 1 couturier, Hardy Amies, later Sir Hardy Amies, to design a new uniform. It was BEA's first significant flight into high-end fashion. Apart from a 1960 design by the then unknown British designer Sylvia Ayton, BEA had approached previous uniform designs in a ready-to-wear rather than made-to-measure fashion. Hardy Amies changed all that, and followed his 1967 design with another in 1972 (which was adopted by British Airways as its inaugural uniform in 1974) and then another for Concorde in 1976.

BEA had realised the potential selling appeal of dressing its 1,500 female customer-facing staff in trendsetting clothes. This was more about people identifying the company as being in line with the times and a leading and distinctive airline. It was an approach similar to that of the 1950s but it went much further. Gone were the dark blues and blacks of the Sylvia Ayton uniform, 1960 chic and 'safe' but hardly inspiring. Hardy Amies designed a vibrant red, white and blue creation, the colours of the Union Flag and BEA's new livery. What better to emphasise BEA's 'Britishness', its 'No. 1' ranking and overall style? Who better to use than Hardy Amies, HM the Queen's couturier, one of London's foremost talents and a consultant menswear designer on a worldwide scale? With many years of experience designing uniforms for sectors as diverse as retailing and the military, Hardy Amies' combination of haute-couture creativity and experience of the practical and financial restraints of designing for a non-retail purpose made him an obvious choice. The latter was a critical factor often overlooked by outsiders. Apart from the design being right and the materials being suitable for a range of situations, financial and practical considerations of cost, durability and the sheer logistics of supply had to be answered.

Hardy Amies' various uniforms endured until 1978, when a new, more formal uniform by the British fashion house Baccarat Weatherall was introduced. By the late 1970s the role of uniformed staff as reflective of British Airways' brand values was considered very important and was much more than just style for its own sake. From a customer perspective, uniformed staff were the front-line troops, the principal members of the airline's staff with whom customers would interact, and often for many hours. How they performed their duties, what they looked like, what they said and how they said it were key to meeting customers' expectations of the British Airways brand promise. The perception was summed up by British Airways' then Deputy Chairman, Sir Henry Marking: 'Our uniformed girls are our best ambassadors and our best advertisements ... It is they who are constantly in the public's eye and it is on them and on their appearance and performance that the airline is often judged so we must ensure that they are always a credit to British Airways.' Apart from missing the fact that the male crew members' performance and appearance mattered just as much (and the rather patronising use of the term 'girls'), Sir Henry was absolutely right. What was interesting was the perception of the Baccarat Weatherall uniform as being 'business-like, attractive yet efficient' – definitely a move away from pure fashion. Some men saw it as rather 'butch' and would have preferred a more feminine style, a view reflective of a past age and no longer appropriate as gender equality moved up the social agenda.

The rather stiff, though necessary, formality of British Airways' uniform regulations lived up to the customer promise standard, but possibly restricted an individual's natural warmth and welcome. The Baccarat Weatherall uniform tried to overcome this limitation by introducing trousers as well as skirts and maintaining a mix-and-match approach to accessories to encourage individuality. Baccarat Weatherall had promised to 'produce a uniform elegant enough to feature in *Vogue*', and Sir Henry added, 'This new outfit will make British Airways' girls the most elegant and attractive in the airline business.'

Fashions from Britain was often about advising passengers what to wear on their journey. As air travel in the 1940s was still a very new transport experience for many people, what to wear abroad featured strongly in advisory passenger brochures for several decades. The rather fussy styles of the 1940s had a marked contrast to the early 1960s *Airwear Everywhere* brochure.

AAGE THAARUP'S *bejewelled and draped black felt tricorne*

ROSE BERTIN'S *wavy brown brim with a tiny bird nestling in the crown of honey-coloured veiling*

STRASSNER'S *long brown and blue tweed jacket flared sharply over a simple brown wool skirt*

HONORE'S *négligée in lime-green moss crepe, cleverly gathered over bust and hips, with a crinkled lamé hem line*

for your journey, Madame . . .

Airwear Everywher

B·O·A·C

Elegance and attractiveness, however, had not been the defining requirements for male uniforms, which had remained almost unchanged from the 1940s to the mid-1980s; while always remaining smart and sometimes even dashing, they had not shown any consistency or obvious relationship to the uniforms of female staff. That all changed in 1985. For the very first time, all British Airways' 25,000 uniformed staff – in the air, on the ground, male and female – were given a new uniform. Designed to reflect the airline's distinctive new corporate identity introduced by Landor Associates, British Airways had, also for the first time, gone outside the UK for a uniform creator. Roland Klein, a French designer who had worked with the likes of Dior and Karl Lagerfeld, stated he had utilised the best elements of the British wardrobe, including classic British garments that the rest of the world had always admired and copied – trench coats, blazers, beautifully tailored skirts and trousers – with a touch of French chic.

In what was almost a turnaround of the Baccarat Weatherall approach, Klein's brief was to produce a uniform that conveyed a less official, less formal image – a new approachable style that complemented British Airways' campaign to 'put the customer first'. As with fashion, the corporate perception of what a uniform should reflect moved to and fro, but the overall direction was toward a much softer, more easy-going style than that of yesteryear.

The Klein uniform was also clearly aligned to British Airways' new corporate image, and was designed in colours of pearl grey, midnight blue and Speedwing red – the 'Speedwing' being Landor's new take on the old 'Speedbird' logo. All well and good, with a clear uniformity across British Airways' brand image, but styles can soon be outdated as trends change. The 1980s-style loose-fitting blouses, draped jackets and long grey skirts with kick pleats, let alone the 'deck-chair' summer outfit, looked good for a while but had no real longevity.

By the early 1990s research among passengers and staff showed that the Klein uniform was considered 'old fashioned' and 'lacking in style'. Not unsurprising in a fashion sense, but it had been intended to last for ten years. Maybe it was just too relaxed? It was not universally liked by female wearers and was rather unforgiving, but it had served well to take British Airways through a period leading to very profitable years and a successful privatisation in January 1987. During the late 1980s, however, a major brand repositioning had been completed that had established the company itself as the centre of its brand family, the masterbrand, the one brand to lead them all.

Brand values had by the early 1990s become part of corporate values, including the 'softer theme of the '90s, with a more sensitive approach to quality of life', all reflected in (another) 'new look'. It's not quite clear what the softer theme of the '90s was, but the new look in 1993 was a new uniform, this time by the Irish designer Paul Costelloe – a blend of casual formality, yet at the same time warm and friendly, a small step back, evoking elegant, classic British quality and style.

Klein had probably gone a bit too '1980s fashionable' in his design, and the changeover to Costelloe cost British Airways £14 million. Changing uniforms does not come cheap! Apart from producing a new design to reflect the airline's corporate values, Costelloe was also concerned with ensuring the materials used were ecologically sound (environmental impacts being a growing concern in the later twentieth century). Wherever possible, natural, renewable fibres and fabrics were used. It was all part of British Airways' brand repositioning to reflect a more human side. In the later years of the 1990s, as part of the company's move to become a global 'twenty-first-century world citizen', cabin crew members were retrained to present an even more informal, less 'British' approach. The Costelloe uniform's blend of casual formality supported this approach, looking good and wearing well into the twenty-first century.

13

BOAC's stewardess in her severe 1940s military-style uniform is in rather stark contrast to the model posing in her light winter outfit aboard a BOAC motor boat. Such boats were used to transport passengers from the quayside to their flying boats moored offshore and some care was necessary to ensure passenger safety, a role traditionally taken by a male rather than a female crew member.

The February 1947 issue of *Picture Post* ran an article called 'A Girl Becomes an Air Steward'. This was no 1940s early attempt at gender equality but a deliberate policy to emphasise that both male and female 'stewards' were equal and up to the task required. Many men still saw women as more decorative and domestic, certainly not the person to be in charge in an emergency. BEA even made the point that the term 'air hostess' was obsolete and plain 'steward' was the word to use. *Picture Post*'s article was somewhere in between, annotating its picture as 'The Comforter of the Skies' and saying, 'She has balance as well as poise. She is polite, but can be stern. She is comforting but not patronising. She is nurse, cook, waitress, librarian and orderly.' Not quite the way to describe the role in the twenty-first century, but the point was being made that in this role women were equal, fully capable and that passengers should be completely reassured.

Right: These three BEA ground staff look more than capable whatever the situation. This picture is from the early 1950s when BEA was moving from its earlier military-style, light-grey uniform (worn by the ground staff to the left and right) to a softer, more feminine, tailored look reflecting the fashions of the time. BEA's new uniform is in the middle and had a rolled collar with a deep revere curving gracefully down to twin buttons at the waistline, which itself was nipped and tucked to reflect the 1950s Christian Dior 'New Look'.

Far right: It is not known who designed the early BEA uniforms. Whatever their origin, the subsequent 'feminising' changes were about introducing both a practical and fashionable style. They had to appear modern, to the extent that the title 'air hostess', not 'steward' was back in vogue by the early 1950s. BEA's air hostess Miss Margaret Eastwood certainly looks fashionable as she 'discusses the latest styles at a fashion house launch'.

Above left: BOAC's dark-blue female uniforms were launched in September 1946 and were not that dissimilar to those worn by BOAC's first 'air stewardesses' during the Second World War. Very military with a collar and tie, they were designed by the UK designer Maurice Helman. His brief was to produce a uniform that would meet 'the practical requirements of airline personnel', nothing too fashionable then, but, like with BEA, it also needed to reflect the airline's professionalism and experience. Helman's take on his brief was to match the need for practicality with a design that was also 'modern, streamlined and typified a spirit of a new machine age'.

Above middle and right: The need to be seen as 'modern' was definitely a key theme in much of 1950s advertising and Helman's design had real longevity, although it was softened in the early 1950s with an open-neck blouse, no belt and was generally made much more feminine in fit and appearance. Apart from modifications by the British couturier Norman Hartnell in the later 1950s, BOAC's uniform lasted up to 1969, when it was replaced by a very new creation styled to reflect the practicalities of the new jet age (the large 747 aircraft was just coming into service) and the contemporary fashion of the time.

Right: BOAC's uniform style was about presenting classic simplicity of design and keeping its 'uniformed girls feminine and in fashion'. Their role was considered a traditional one for a woman, i.e. a supporting role. As well as the usual preparation and serving of food, they had 'special responsibilities', defined as 'looking after children and aged or unwell passengers; for keeping tidy the cabin and cloakrooms and for helping to create a pleasant, relaxed atmosphere'. The chief steward was always a man – how times have changed.

Far right: By the late 1960s, BOAC's advertising had become more light-hearted, rather reflective of the less serious 1960s. 'Our flighty birds' goes too far from a gender perspective, but it was a sign of the times.

On the Trans-Pacific Routes, Japanese and
Chinese stewardesses add a charm and courtesy of their
own to the golden legend of B.O.A.C. cabin service.

This spread: In the mid-1950s, BOAC introduced national dress uniforms for its Chinese, Indian, Pakistani and Japanese services. White cheongsams, colourful saris and traditional kimonos were worn by national stewardesses from these countries who spoke the relevant languages and understood the associated cultures. It was an extension of BOAC's 'taking more care' approach on routes with which it had strong historic links, and it was a service enhancement much appreciated by passengers.

BOAC

No. 25   AUTUMN 1970

cabin crew bulletin

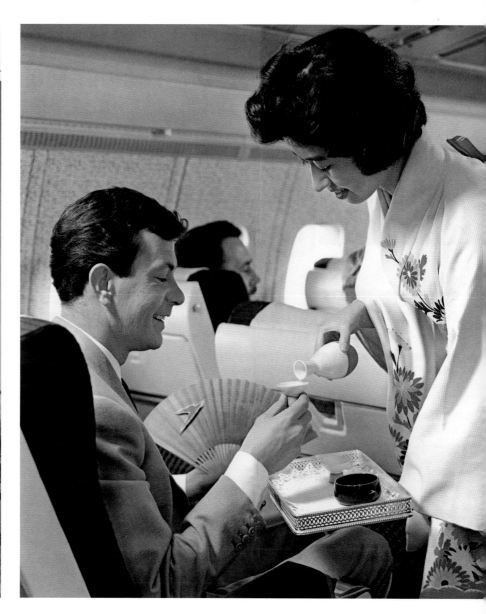

Left: Japanese stewardess Mie Ogahara wears a red michiyuki coat that was introduced on the UK–Japan polar route in 1969. The kimonos were not designed for and issued by BOAC – each Japanese stewardess was given a set amount of money to buy a kimono of their choice from their local shops, the only stipulation being that it must be of a traditional pattern and design. Ms Ogahara was the 1967 'Miss Tourism for Japan' before joining BOAC the following year.

Below and opposite: Apart from its completely contrasted dark-blue/black check pattern, Sylvia Ayton's design is not that far away from BEA's earlier light-grey creation. A slightly shorter straight skirt, wide collar (buttoned to the neck this time) and a modified hat without a cockade, it was all 1960s chic and very smart, befitting one of the UK's nationalised airlines. The more flamboyant styles of the later 1960s were yet to come. Male uniforms, however, continued along the usual traditional lines – dark blues or black, single or double breasted, four gold rings for the captain. Things would hardly change either for BOAC or BEA male crews and ground staff until 1984, at the end of British Airways' first decade.

BEA

Your flight
Safety on board
see pages
2, 3, 4 & 5

For you to keep

Votre vol
Sécurité
à bord
voir pages
2, 3, 4 & 5

Gardez cette brochure

Ihr Flug
Sicherheit
an Bord
siehe Seiten
2, 3, 4 & 5

Bitte mitnehmen

When approached by BEA in 1966 to design a new uniform, Hardy Amies said, 'I am very pleased to design new uniforms for this great national airline. BEA carries more passengers than any other airline in Europe and provides an excellent shop window for British fashion.' However, being a vehicle to promote British fashion was not uppermost in BEA's thoughts when they decided to take a more couture approach to their new uniform. They had done all that in the 1940s and while it was fine as a spin-off, the first and foremost purpose was to promote BEA. The Sylvia Ayton uniform had kept BEA fashionable for a few years, but its benefit was short-lived, with fashions changing fast as the 1960s progressed at a rapid social pace.

Hardy Amies' uniform certainly was a flight into fashion. The design focussed on the three primary colours of red (particularly the very striking caped overcoat), royal blue for the jacket and dress and white for the blouse and gloves. It matched BEA's new livery, particularly its aircraft's red wings, and was, of course, the colours of the Union Flag and very appropriate for a national airline. The new uniform certainly made BEA stand out from the crowd and any associations with Little Red Riding Hood were purely incidental.

 MAGAISZNE

BEA

No. 227
Price 3d.

MAY
1968

Top left and right: BOAC took its own flight into 'flower power' fashion in 1967 with an in-house design of a paper dress for its flights between New York and the Caribbean. Manufactured by Joseph Lore Inc. in the USA, bonded paper clothing was a new idea for cheap, disposable wear and BOAC's paper dress uniforms were intended to be only worn once and then discarded.

Bottom left: BOAC stewardess Pat Bleasdale models the paper dress uniform at its media launch in October 1966. The dresses may have helped put passengers into a holiday mood as they travelled south to the Caribbean, and they did put BOAC into the fashion limelight for a very short while, but the fad did not last and the dresses were withdrawn after less than a year. Legend has it that some high-spirited (male) passengers were tempted to take a cigarette lighter to the dress to see what would happen!

**all-new BOAC uniform
for the all-new BOAC 747**

DESIGNED BY CLIVE, one of London's most exciting young couturiers, a brand-new BOAC uniform makes its first appearance aboard the new BOAC 747. Immensely smart, as well as practical and versatile, the new BOAC uniform for stewardesses meets every need. Ideal for arctic winds as well as tropical heat. Dress and jacket *(terylene and wool worsted)* stays eternally spotless with detachable drip dry white collar. Boots and a warm wool top-coat go over the Pole in style. Tropical dress is wilt-proof terylene and cotton twill, drip dry.

This spread: In 1969 BOAC had taken delivery of its first 747 aircraft and also introduced an entirely new uniform. Up-and-coming British designer Clive Evans had done well to win the tender from Mary Quant and Jean Muir, both leading UK designers of 1960s fashion. Clive's new uniform was certainly very different from its predecessor and very much reflected both practicality and the new 'London Look'. The theme of practicality first and fashion second had by now become the defining approach to BOAC's (and BEA's) uniform designs. With much greater numbers of passengers on the 747 and the demands of both Arctic winds and tropical steam heat, the uniform ensemble certainly needed to be practical but also needed to look good and be aligned to the fashion of the time. The summer uniform in Caribbean blue or coral pink was certainly easy-wear and practical, being made from terylene and cotton twill, and was washable in a hotel sink to drip-dry overnight. The winter dress and jacket in terylene and wool worsted was also easy-care and stayed immaculate whatever the weather threw at it.

BOAC stewardesses world-wide will wear the new uniform, which makes its first appearance aboard the BOAC 747

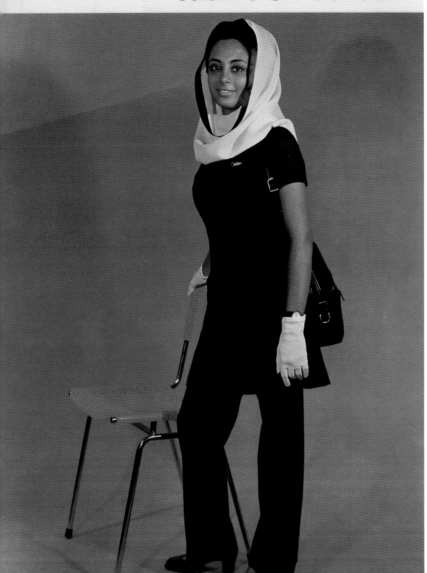

BOAC

No. 30 SPRING 1972 cabin crew bulletin

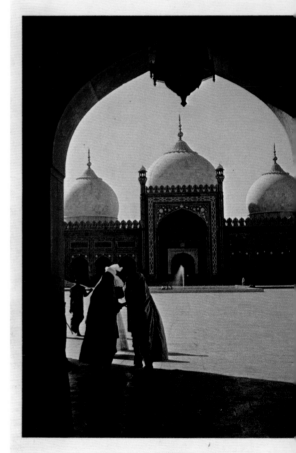

Pakista

Clive also adapted his
new uniform to introduce
a new look for BOAC's
Pakistani stewardesses.
A navy-blue tunic with
matching trousers and
white georgette hood
was introduced, styled to
conform to a modified
type of national costume,
worn here (left) by
stewardess Eileen Carson.

BOAC

In 1972, only five years after introducing its first Hardy Amies uniform, BEA replaced it entirely with another Hardy Amies creation. This was a surprising move given the earlier design remained fashionable, smart and was well-liked by staff and passengers. Replacing an entire uniform is also an expensive exercise and not taken lightly. One thing the earlier BEA uniform did not reflect, however, was any brand relationship with BOAC, soon to be merged with BEA in 1974. The colours were patriotic but were nothing like BOAC's more formal white and dark blue and were a mile away from the summery tropical style of the Clive Evans' creation introduced by BOAC only two years earlier.

Hardy Amies' new uniform looked rather like a compromise. It was mainly in dark blue with touches of red flashing and interchangeable blouses in white, red or blue. A beige trench coat replaced the red overcoat and, one might argue, it was more BOAC than BEA, at least in cut and colour. Describing it as 'elegant and feminine', Hardy Amies also reasoned that 'there is a strong current trend away from uniformity, especially amongst the young, so I have designed a uniform which does allow the expression of individuality'. It was very smart and stylish, but that and the wish to introduce individuality was not really a strong enough reason to incur the considerable expense of a uniform changeover. From a Machiavellian perspective, it might be questioned whether the move was more to do with trying to ensure that BEA's new uniform and not BOAC's was adopted by the new British Airways when it was formed. BEA management are believed not to have liked the Clive Evans' creation, and whether by fair means or foul (apart from changing the badges and keeping the Clive Evans' summer uniform for hot climates), the Hardy Amies uniform prevailed.

Concorde was so very different from anything that had gone before that it just had to have a new uniform for its cabin crews, or at least that was the idea. Who else but Hardy Amies to offer a design, and not just for the twentieth but for the twenty-first century, both in style and colour? The space film *Close Encounters of the Third Kind* would not be released until 1977, but Concorde's launch in 1976 was almost a preview, not least in what the cabin crew were wearing. Pale blue was the predominant colour for a design that would not have been out of place in the world's dance halls let alone the aircraft's cabin. The uniform was worn on the first service from London to Bahrain on 26 January 1976, but was withdrawn after a six-month trial. It was not that it did not meet its brief, but it was very elitist, and the company did not want the Concorde crews to be seen as any more elitist than they were likely to become. As it was, the Baccarat Weatherall pinstripe uniform introduced just two years later more than took its place on what became known as the Concorde 'businessman's special'.

This spread: In 1978 British Airways introduced its very first uniform. No longer a hand-me-down from its predecessor airline BEA, the Baccarat Weatherall fashion house design certainly made a fashion statement with its lightweight, dark-blue, pinstriped, wool worsted jacket, skirt and trouser alternative. A lightweight PVC raincoat was an innovation, but the real change was the small-brimmed hats – as the media said they were 'getting ahead with hats' and it added 'more than a touch of class and more than a touch of British style'. Concorde had just entered service two years earlier and the style complemented the aircraft beautifully, or was it the other way around? If anything, the introduction of the Baccarat Weatherall uniform was the beginning of the first public manifestation of the new British Airways and its brand values. They had not been expressed in that way yet, but in terms of style and promise the company strongly met customers' expectations. Although British Airways had several years of hard work ahead of it to even begin to meet its business objectives and financial expectations, its brand image was beginning to become established.

Hela världen via London

British airways

Sketch B   Sketch C

Roland Klein's intention was to design an 'updated timelessness' into his British Airways uniform, not least to ensure it lasted around ten years, a broad rule of thumb for uniform longevity. Klein believed the Baccarat Weatherall uniform was 'too tight, structured and stiff' and that the 1980s was all about a softer image. Style and cut were certainly important factors in the previous decade, but Klein's new uniform still needed to be strongly corporate to complement British Airways new and very corporate livery.

Klein successfully bridged the two ideals, at least in terms of the male uniforms. For the first time, silver braid replaced the traditional gold, very much a break with the past as gold had denoted rank since the 1920s. Klein also went much further than before in the totality of his uniform range. It covered all uniformed staff across the airline, male, female, on the ground and in the air. It even included national crew uniforms with new saris, a cheongsam and a traditional salwar kameez-style uniform for Pakistani cabin crew. The kimonos had gone in 1974 at the request of the Japanese cabin crew, who no longer wanted to wear a traditional dress that, while distinctive, was difficult to wear on duty.

British Airways' Concorde stewardesses Elaine and Estelle Moffat, aka the 'supersonic twins', wearing the Klein uniform – a rather unique pairing.

The Klein uniform stands out as a real break with the past. It linked the whole airline together in a common corporate style and was seen by management at the time as one of the most important elements of British Airways' corporate image. Widely used in advertising and associated publicity material, it did look good at the right time and in the right place and on the right people, but life, especially business life, can never be that perfect.

Possibly one of the world's most distinctive stewardess uniforms was that introduced by Caledonian Airways, the forerunner of British Caledonian Airways (BCAL), in the 1960s. Made from eight authentic Scottish clan tartans and a ninth non-clan tartan, the 'Dress Black Watch', Caledonian Airways were ahead of their day in encouraging individuality and identity, with more than a nod towards Scottish heritage. Anything but 'uniform', stewardesses could choose from either 'Graham of Monteith', 'MacKellar', 'Red MacDuff', 'MacInnes', 'Hunting MacRae', 'Kennedy', 'Hunting Ogilvie' or 'MacNab', but if none of these was her own clan tartan or if she preferred to wear a neutral one, the 'Dress Black Watch' tartan could be chosen.

BCAL was merged with British Airways in 1988 and earlier that year had introduced a new tartan uniform based on a common design, the 'Princess Mary' tartan. Fashioned in six colours – rose, navy, blue, green, grey and black – each stewardess could choose two of the colours, again to encourage individuality. These uniforms continued to be used by the Caledonian Airways charter subsidiary of British Airways until it was sold in 1995.

The 'Caledonian Girls', as the stewardesses became known, were a key element of the BCAL brand identity. Although stylish, the tartan uniforms were nothing to do with current fashion but a striking feature of the airline's corporate identity and tribute to Scottish heritage. It was also still very much a man's world in BCAL: female tartan trousers ('trews') were not permitted.

The most striking part of the Paul Costelloe uniform was its 'Aztec'-design blouse and matching summer skirt. Made from polyester crêpe de Chine, it was easy-care and draped beautifully, keeping the skirt's multiple pleats razor sharp. Together with the stylish formal jacket with its tiny pin-dot design, it really was a blend of casual sophistication that presented a professional but approachable image at all times. Costelloe was very aware that 'a uniform isn't just something you wear, it's got to support you in your job', and that means keeping that professional look but being comfortable and practical at all times, whatever the weather and travel conditions. It was very forgiving and suited most wearers, and even the boater-style hat flattered all shapes of face.

The 'Aztec' design itself was an unintended example of the 'World Images' livery designs yet to come in 1997, and it worked very well as a combination of understated 'British' style with a cosmopolitan flair. The Costelloe uniform was a key part of the British Airways brand promise throughout the 1990s and early 2000s. It took the company through a difficult period adjusting to its attempt to become a twenty-first-century world citizen, and the subsequent change to its corporate livery to focus on the Chatham Flag design as the central part of its new masterbrand.

Not designed by Paul Costelloe but by the Indian designers Abu Jani and Sandeep Khosla, a new sari was introduced in 1996 on British Airways' India and Bangladesh services. In a design true to Indian culture and matching Costelloe's Western uniform design in corporate red, white and blue, British Airways stewardess Manisha Kohli, a former Miss India, strikes a traditional welcoming pose in the image to the right..

BRITISH AIRWAYS

Calcutta

INDIA

The only direct service
from London Heathrow

7

CLIMBING ABOVE THE TURBULENCE

At the end of the 1990s, British Airways set itself a rather daunting challenge – to redefine air travel and set a course for the new millennium. In what would be promoted as 'twenty-first-century air travel', the 'World Images' branding would fade away and all aircraft would progressively be repainted and emerge in the Chatham Flag livery, the new masterbrand livery with its associated 'Speedmarque' logo. The twenty-first-century air-travel initiative would, however, continue the theme of art, principally in photography, but also by illustrating each product brand benefit in an inspirational and evocative way, a sort of 'state-of-the-art air-travel' theme. This was more about using art as an illustrative advertising medium than as an integral brand component, as 'World Images' had attempted. The 1990s had seen the masterbrand aligned with British Airways' global strategy; twenty-first-century air travel was about realigning it with the company's business strategy and placing service excellence at its heart.

The aim of the realignment was very clear: 'World Images' as a brand concept had been a diversion. The only image worthy of continued service was the Chatham Flag livery, and that suited British Airways' modern British image. Service excellence was emphasised as 'rooted in our heritage and at the core of everything we do and the way we behave', and was 'a clear platform from which to plan a bright future'. The twenty-first century also saw a shift in focus towards British Airways' most valuable customers, mainly those travelling in First and Club World, placing even greater emphasis on prestige and premium values. They also concentrated on the key points of difference between the company and its competitors,

those things that made it unique. Service excellence in both people and products was therefore considered to lie at the heart of the British Airways brand and was 'the key differentiator that drives consumer choice'. How this service excellence was delivered was what made the company unique and recognisable, and underpinning delivery were the core brand values: modern British, innovative, high standards, reassuring and professional.

Service excellence and a drive on premium business may have been intended as a clear brand platform for a bright future, but it was essentially a focus on the most profitable long-haul side of the business, although customers travelling in Club Europe, British Airways' short-haul business class, also made a valuable contribution. Short-haul generally, mainly the UK–Europe Euro Traveller economy market, BEA's old hunting grounds and always a difficult market to make money in, was being eroded by the rise of the (mainly) UK low-cost airlines that were encouraged by the UK's open-competition policy and more flexible European Union rules on route entry. Not since the introduction of the Club Europe and Euro Traveller product brands in the late 1980s had British Airways invested any real effort in trying to make its European product brands stand out, even though its Europe market share had been over 30 per cent in the late 1990s and a high percentage of its long-haul feeder traffic.

The economic recession of 2000/01, aggravated by the shock to world civil aviation caused by the 9/11 terrorist attack, led British Airways to review its whole business structure. 'Future Size and Shape' was the name of the resulting survival plan, a plan on a scale of that of the early 1980s. This

Previous page and left: The core elements of the British Airways masterbrand for the twenty-first century: the Chatham Flag tailfin marking a return to a stylised Union Flag to emphasise the airline's British origins together with the 'Speedmarque' logo or signature in red and silver, a flash of energy and sophistication, a visual indicator of service quality and status.

Below: State-of-the-art air travel was certainly a different approach to promoting the benefits of the British Airways brands. Apart from the usual glossy brochure product images, the lead-in page image for the World Traveller seat product was a picture of the artwork entitled '**That's** entertainment'. The accompanying text read, 'Allow yourself to become absorbed by the World Traveller experience as new seat-back video screens distract the eye and occupy the mind', which '**That's** entertainment' certainly did. (Mark Reddick)

time there would be no government rescue and no certainty shareholders would inject capital as the share price dropped alarmingly low and the airline was ejected from the FTSE 100 group of companies. British Airways' Chief Executive, Rod Eddington, summarised the basis of the plan: 'We will remain true to our heritage of being a full-service network carrier, committed to customer service excellence and world-class products but we must transform British Airways into a simpler, leaner, more focussed airline so we can thrive and prosper in an increasingly competitive market.' The issue was not product but price, and that meant standards had to be maintained, even improved, but within stricter cost controls so that shareholder value could still be achieved and provide a return to allow future product and service investment.

Across the company a target was set of a 10 per cent operating margin and annualised cost savings of £650 million by March 2004; staff cuts, mostly voluntary, were also anticipated. Overall, capacity was to be cut by 21 per cent but slashed by 60 per cent at Gatwick. Nearly fifty aircraft were to leave the fleet. A particular focus was placed on UK regional and European services, the fight-back against the low-cost airlines. This was very much about a complete overhaul of short-haul pricing to provide lower fares, greater flexibility and more choice while continuing to offer all the benefits of a full-service airline, that is, free meals, baggage, online check-in, city airports, etc. Some argued that such 'frills' were unnecessary on short routes, things paid for but not needed, but they were, in effect, the basis of the value many consumers saw in the British Airways brand. What was critical was getting the message across that 'frills' equalled 'service that matters', something British Airways could deliver that the others by their nature could not. This message did not change the masterbrand or associated product brands in any major way, but it did change the way they were communicated and promoted by highlighting their overall value. This was a key point, as once all the low-cost airlines' add-on fees were included, flying with them could actually be more expensive. On British Airways the 'extras' came free, as did its brand promise to perform time and time again.

Despite cost-cutting elsewhere, British Airways' short-haul advertising spend went into overdrive to provide relentless communication on television, radio, print and outdoor media. The aim was to stand out from the competition and achieve a clear shift in the public's perception of the airline – it could be a viable travel option for short-haul leisure travellers. What was particularly noticeable was the use of online media through the 2002–04 period, a deliberate approach used to create a long-term campaign presence using the rapidly growing digital format and to drive online sales. Such advertising made the sale by driving prospective customers to ba.com, the British Airways website, and not a telephone number as before. This reduced selling costs, an imperative if British Airways was to succeed in the low-cost market. It showed the power of advertising in changing not only customers' perceptions but also their habits. Bookings on ba.com rose over 20 per cent in the first two years of the campaign, and this shift to online bookings continued.

By 2004 British Airways was back among the world's top twenty airlines in terms of overall profit; short-haul losses had been reduced to £26 million that year, a tenth of the figure it had been at the turn of the millennium. The drive to stay in Europe was working, but a lot more effort was required to maintain and increase passenger numbers and become profitable. The silver lining to a major upgrade in the British Airways' customer experience was also still four years away, as Heathrow Terminal 5 was only half built, but it promised a significant improvement, tantalisingly now just on the horizon.

A more immediate silver lining was a major change to the customer-facing staff in the form of a new uniform by the British fashion designer Julien Macdonald, which was launched in 2004. Julien Macdonald was a surprise choice given his controversial reputation for 'glitzy' and glamorous designs, but bringing a bit of glamour back was what

British Airways wanted, although not along the lines of 'Cool Britannia' or 'sparkly Union Jacks', which had sometimes been attributed to his work. This was more about a new uniform for the new millennium and a break with the past, albeit with a 'classic, modern, stylish but practical' design. Importantly, it was to reflect the airline's 'Britishness', now firmly seen as a virtue and an important part of British Airways' overall brand values. The new uniform was internally described as 'representing a sharp, modern silhouette with a respectful nod to our heritage'. It was at once 'British' and professional looking, yet had a softer touch – everything British Airways wanted to reflect in its core values. It was safe and secure, thoughtful, warm, responsible, professional and British. There was an emphasis on being 'warm and thoughtful', clearly tuning into customers' needs and genuinely connecting with them, the sort of warm and thoughtful approach that makes for a great service and a great airline. This was not a return to the late 1990s attempt to be a 'world citizen', but was a genuine move to provide the sort of empathetic, welcoming and friendly customer service style that customers expected. This and more would be needed, as within the next twelve months the airline industry faced its worst ever trading environment as a major world recession took hold and oil prices doubled.

BRITISH AIRWAYS

ot just refined,
redefined

...ver how **British Airways**
is revolutionising the air travel experience

21st Century Air Travel

This spread: Not just refined but redefined – British Airways was certainly revolutionising the air travel experience at the turn of the millennium with a £600 million programme of product and service enhancements. Probably most important was the new Club World seat, a first in the industry and way ahead of the competition due to its revolutionary patented design that allowed the passenger seat to unfold into a fully flat, six-foot bed within its own seat housing. In a so-called 'Ying-Yang' configuration, the new seat was a considerable step up in comfort and privacy, almost on a par with First. Quite why the advert includes an image of a bathroom is not clear. The new seat did many things but it did not convert into a bathroom. (Right: MCSaatchi)

Club World. More beds, more places, more often. BRITISH AIRWAYS

Club World. More beds, more places, more often. BRITISH AIRWAYS

Club World. More beds, more places, more often. BRITISH AIRWAYS

Club World. More beds, more places, more often. BRITISH AIRWAYS

Club World. More beds, more places, more often. BRITISH AIRWAYS

A flying start.

British Airways presents a new dimension on premium economy travel:
World Traveller Plus with 7 inches more legroom.

oneworld member

BRITISH AIRWAYS

you

Seat 28b

World Traveller Plus was a new product introduced in 2000 as part of British Airways' twenty-first-century redefinition, another recognition of the demand from many business and leisure travellers who wanted a little more space and comfort but at affordable prices. World Traveller Plus customers would enjoy a spacious, quieter new economy class in a completely separate cabin with wider seats and more legroom, and this has become a very popular choice.

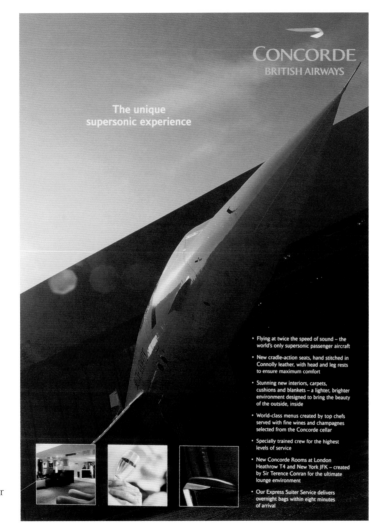

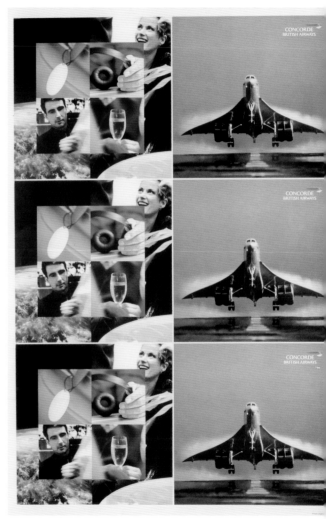

Concorde was the ultimate travel experience and rather defined both twentieth- and twenty-first-century air travel. It had its own enhancements aimed at maintaining the sort of ultra-luxury experience expected by its clientele. In truth, no matter what was done to the 'time machine', as it was called, it hardly ever failed to meet its customers' expectations. (MCSaatchi)

The First cabin interior was given a makeover by Kelly Hoppen in 2001, who gave a touch of her own personal style to the cabin, giving it almost a 'lounge (or bedroom) in the sky' feeling. Wood finishes, plush upholstery and cushioning together with thoughtful and discreet service made First customers feel very much at home.

Unmistakably FIRST

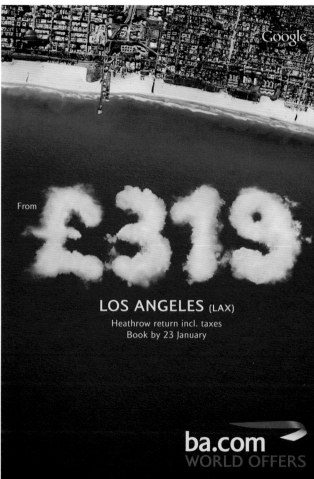

Above and right: Low prices and with all the 'frills' included, British Airways' answer to the low-cost short-haul airlines. (MCSaatchi)

Far right: Low long-haul prices had also become a regular response to the ups and downs of the air travel business under the British Airways 'World Offers' promotions. (Bartle Bogle Hegarty/Google Earth)

Julien Macdonald certainly has a couture pedigree as former artistic director for the House of Givenchy in Paris and head knitwear designer at Chanel. His designs are highly sophisticated, glamorous and elegant and he has applied the same philosophy to the current British Airways uniform, resulting in a sharp, modern silhouette with a respectful nod to its heritage. Female cabin crew have a choice of wearing skirts or trousers in a navy pinstripe wool fabric, complemented by a white blouse with red detailing and a bespoke patterned cravat worn under a smart fitted jacket with silver buttons. Celebrated British milliner Stephen Jones designed the hat. The male and female flight crew uniforms continue the trend introduced by Roland Klein for silver braid rank markings that rather emphasise that cool assurance and 'dash' that only a uniform can imply.

Designed by the Indian fashion designer Rohit Bal, a kurta-style dress with a sherwani tunic was introduced in 2007 for British Airways' Indian female cabin crew to replace the traditional saris. Designed as an interpretation of the Julien Macdonald uniform but reflecting Indian culture, the kurta is now used on all British Airways routes worldwide – worn here by Neha Pandey with Gaurav Gogia in his Julian Macdonald uniform.

11 flights a day to New York **BRITISH AIRWAYS**

Above: The Statue of Liberty has always provided an iconic image for advertisers everywhere, not least in 2006 when it gave British Airways' new advertising agency, Bogle Bartle Hegarty, an opportunity to use the statue's pointed crown to emphasise the airline's eleven flights a day to New York, a marked contrast to its predecessor BOAC's four services a week sixty years earlier. (Bartle Bogle Hegarty)

Middle and right: British Airways' membership of the **one**world alliance now gives prominence in many adverts to its logo, which also figures prominently on the fuselages of nine of the airline's fleet of 747 aircraft. (Bottom right: James Davies)

If only packing
was as simple
as checking in
from home.

ba.com

BRITISH AIRWAYS

Seeing stars.
Visit London
by night.

Book now at **ba.com**

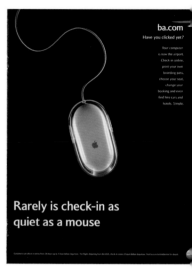

ba.com

Have you clicked yet?

Rarely is check-in as
quiet as a mouse

British Airways' website,
ba.com, has rapidly become
the single biggest contact point
for its customers worldwide,
one of the most sophisticated
internet travel sites and a key
component of its brand promise.
The occasional difficulties
of checking in have been
transformed online – 'rarely is
check-in as quiet as a mouse'.
(Bartle Bogle Hegarty)

8

BRINGING IT ALL TOGETHER

The opening of London Heathrow Terminal 5 in March 2008 was widely anticipated to be the next big thing in developing the British Airways customer experience and its brand promise to perform. Its debut was a high-profile disappointment, although not solely of the airline's making, and what emerged in the following weeks was a steely determination to make it work. It was all about performance, that key ingredient of the brand promise whose elements were central to the perception of British Airways as an airline that stood out and could be relied upon and trusted. From a hesitant start, Terminal 5's operations rapidly got into gear, improving performance scores across all services. The message that Terminal 5 was working and providing a high-quality travel experience became the subject of an award-winning advertising campaign in August 2008. 'Try it for yourself', the advert said, and many millions of customers did, to their great satisfaction.

The challenges of 2008 did not end with Terminal 5's performance improvement. The next two years brought the most severe trading conditions British Airways had ever faced as the world economy slid into the worst recession since the 1930s, forcing structural change throughout the commercial aviation world. Over thirty-five airlines stopped operating or merged with others, including several major national airlines, but competition increased from new entrants and established airlines, particularly the European low-cost airlines and those from the Middle East.

Consolidation was expected to be a major theme for the foreseeable future, and it would have to happen at an accelerating pace. Price, product and performance would be centre stage more than ever in winning over customers, but more was necessary to protect both the British Airways brand promise and to achieve a permanent change in its cost base. The airline's membership of the **one**world alliance would help, and its brand reach had been extended through a careful use of alliances and franchises, but it needed a more structural approach to bring increased financial strength to accelerate investment in new products and services.

In January 2011, airline partnerships took on a new meaning as British Airways and Iberia Airlines of Spain joined together under a new parent company, International Airlines Group (IAG). This was a very attractive deal from a whole range of perspectives, bringing Iberia's Latin American network to complement British Airways' global reach and to further strengthen the **one**world alliance. Both airlines would, however, continue to operate separately and maintain their own brands, with IAG setting strategy and driving the expected huge synergy benefits. This was a critical change: not only would the British Airways brand promise be strengthened, but the airline could now focus solely on its performance, product and service offerings – the all-important 'doing business' and customer satisfaction parts of its operation. With the glimmerings of the end of the recession, it was also not the time to be initiating a major rebranding exercise as British Airways had had to do on its formation in 1974. Research had highlighted the overall strength of the British Airways brand – it was well known and highly respected across the world. The fundamentals of the business had been addressed following the 'Future

Size and Shape' restructuring, lowering the airline's costs and improving performance. These were things the company had had to do to survive, but the requirements would remain a constant for its future.

Standing out from the crowd became an undisputed reality for British Airways in September 2011 with the launch of its first major brand advertising campaign for many years. Considered by some to be 'a tipping point for social media's importance to the advertising world', the campaign launched on Facebook – the first big brand launch of a major advertising campaign on social media. The whole script was a narrative about pioneering, acknowledging British Airways' rich heritage over nine decades in a flying sequence that was both evocative and cutting-edge, on a par with the 'Manhattan is landing' campaign of the early 1980s in its scale and originality, a 'cinematic tour-de-force'. This campaign was not only about attracting new business but strengthening the loyalty of existing customers under a renewal of the British Airways brand promise. This promise was expressed as 'To Fly. To Serve.', a reiteration of the old motto that was part of the airline's original heraldic coat of arms. Keith Williams, British Airways' then CEO and now Executive Chairman, had emphasised it was 'important we refocus our efforts on those we serve', and what sets British Airways apart from other airlines – British style, thoughtful service and flying know-how – the three pillars that underpinned the renewed brand promise.

The long-term vision for British Airways is to become the most admired airline. Admired for who it is and what it does by customers, competitors, the communities it serves and all its stakeholders. This is a very ambitious idea. The steps toward it are known internally as 'Our Plan' – a careful use of the term to emphasise it is not just a business plan for management but one for everyone in the company. 'Our Plan' very much brings out the essence of British Airways and its brand promise to deliver 'British style, thoughtful service and flying know-how'. Delivering operational

This spread and next page: 'Bringing people together this Christmas' was part of British Airways' December 2007 advertising campaign. With just over three months to its expected opening, using Heathrow Terminal 5 in the campaign seemed an opportunity too good to miss. The idea was to get across the warmth of the season and demonstrate how British Airways brings people together. Eight months later the airline was having to advertise that 'Terminal 5 is working' to overcome the initial public perception that it was not delivering on its customer promise. It was actually doing much more than that, and by any measure of performance it has enhanced the British Airways customer experience to new levels of satisfaction. The shopping is pretty good too. (Bartle Bogle Hegarty)

excellence and outstanding service is a critical cornerstone, coupled with the plan's £5 billion investment in aircraft, product and technology. In 2014, British Airways was voted the leading consumer Superbrand in the UK, judged as a 'testament to the goodwill felt towards it and the depth of consumers' emotional connection'. It was the first time the accolade had been bestowed on an airline or on any travel industry company – a remarkable achievement, particularly given the strength of the world-class consumer brands competing for the award.

IN AUGUST THE 7,000,000th CUSTOMER FLEW THROUGH T5

Seven million is the number of people who have arrived at, or departed from London Heathrow Terminal 5 since it opened in March. That's the equivalent of almost the entire population of Switzerland jetting off on holiday.
ba.com/t5

BRITISH AIRWAYS

Terminal 5 is working
Try it for yourself

BRITISH AIRWAYS

**TERMINAL 5
A DESTINATION IN ITSELF**

Breezy transits, quiet efficiency and superb shopping. It's the home of British Airways.

To Fly. To Serve.

CARRY ON!

SHOPPING AT
TERMINAL 5
HEATHROW

oneworld

This and next page: Despite constant cost pressures, serious investment capital was being spent on new developments across the British Airways product brand range in the later 2000s. Announced in 2006 and progressively implemented across the long-haul fleet, a £100 million programme of improvements to Club World was introduced, followed two years later by another £100 million announced for First. By 2010 as the First rollout began it was quickly followed by improvements to both the World Traveller Plus and World Traveller product brands. (Bartle Bogle Hegarty)

BRITISH AIRWAYS

Exceptional comfort in refined surroundings

Relax in your personal suite offering you ultimate comfort and balanced privacy. From the moment you book to the moment you arrive at your destination, First delivers exclusive luxury with the finest attention to detail.

Discover more at **ba.com/first**

The plane doesn't fly any faster when you're in Club World. It just seems that way.

Discover more at **ba.com/clubworld**

BRITISH AIRWAYS

Taking care of the whole family

Keeping your little ones happy means you'll be happy too. Healthy and nutritious meals are served on board, and your children will be occupied for hours thanks to dedicated in-flight entertainment.

Discover more at **ba.com/worldtraveller**

BRITISH AIRWAYS

BRITISH AIRWAYS
World Traveller

Have a comfortable journey, you're in good hands

You're in good hands when you fly with British Airways World Traveller, our economy class cabin. We'll do everything we can to ensure you have a smooth and comfortable journey, so you can just sit back, relax and enjoy what's on offer.

BRITISH AIRWAYS

To recline. To sleep.
To lie flat across
our entire fleet.
To Fly. To Serve.

We offer the only truly flat bed in
business to over 50 destinations.
Along with a memory foam
headrest and quilted luxury blanket,
to ensure you sleep like a dream.

Left: It makes a great ad, but wearing one's nightdress is entirely optional in Club World. (Bartle Bogle Hegarty)

Below and next page: Just ahead of the formation of IAG was the announcement of regulatory clearance for the long-awaited Atlantic alliance between British Airways, American Airlines and Iberia. This was all about linking the combined strengths of the three airlines to offer major improvements in customer benefits, over 1,000 flat beds a day between London and New York in 2014 being a notable example. It would not change the look and feel of each airline's brand, and no aircraft would be painted in the advert's rather fanciful montage, but it would be a major improvement to the ease with which customers could travel across the three airlines' combined networks, almost as if they were one airline. (Next page: Bartle Bogle Hegarty)

NEW! JOINT BUSINESS

BRITISH AIRWAYS

ATLANTIC ALLIANCE

Preparing for take off – our new airline tie up, ready to give our competitors a run for their money

BRITISH AIRWAYS

NEVER UNDERESTIMATE THE POWER OF A GOOD FLIGHT'S SLEEP.

Over 1,000 flat beds between
London and New York every day, together with American Airlines.

Book now at ba.com. To Fly. To Serve.

oneworld

'Bringing it all together' was a neat summation at the time of the value of the synergies to be gained by joining together the reach and strength of British Airways' and Iberia's brands under the umbrella of IAG ownership. 'Tying the knot' was another way of expressing it, but this was more of a partnership than a marriage. Both airlines would continue to operate as separate brands, with separate products and even service style, but a gradual interweaving and joining together of common functions has begun to soften the edges between the two companies. Forty years earlier BOAC and BEA had been pressed into a forced marriage to form British Airways as one company. It took nearly ten years for that model to begin delivering on its brand promise, but IAG has no such luxury in the highly competitive twenty-first-century commercial aviation world. Just three years later, the IAG promise is delivering substantial savings and anticipated operating profits in 2014 of over £1.3 billion.

TYING THE KNOT

As our merger with Iberia gets the green light, we look at what the creation of our new airline group means for BA, colleagues and customers

oneworld

TO FLY. TO SERVE.

These four words were painted on
our early aircraft. And our pilots still
wear them with pride. In the lining
of their jackets and on the peaks of
their hats. They're rarely noticed,
but they've always been at the heart
of everything we do. Because they're
not a slogan. They're a promise.
Today, we're committing to our promise
again. Investing more than £5bn in
new aircraft, smarter cabins, elegant
lounges, and new technologies to
make life more comfortable in the
air and on the ground. This is just the
start, and we'll continue to build
on our promise. With the confidence
that we face our future with the same
pride we feel for our past.

To Fly. To Serve.
It's what we do. It's who we are.

In June 2011 a new, five-year, £5 billion business plan was unveiled, aimed at British Airways becoming 'the most admired airline across the world's key cities'. This was much more than just spending money on products, and very much went back to basics in terms of achieving key brand expectations, in particular about winning customers through outstanding service and 'reigniting' passion and belief in the British Airways brand. In other words, delivering great service with a personal touch. This was about much more than products and planes, it was about delivering on that customer promise to perform, putting the customer back at the heart of the business and meeting the high customer expectations associated with the British Airways brand as a whole.

The business plan effectively launched British Airways' new brand campaign aimed at telling the world what the company stood for, including a renewal of its brand promise expressed as 'To Fly. To Serve.', a visual representation of what sets British Airways apart from other airlines: British style, thoughtful service and flying know-how – the three pillars that underpin the new brand promise. (Bartle Bogle Hegarty)

In the top image, BOAC's VC10 aircraft line up preparing to board, an uncanny replication of a scene of nearly fifty years ago thanks to computer-generated images in the background and some original heritage props from the time. 'Aviators' was a Bartle Bogle Hegarty advertising tour-de-force for British Airways. The final scene sums up the heritage theme, the ninety-five years of service that make British Airways what it is today and underpins its customer service promise encapsulated in the words 'To Fly. To Serve.' (Bartle Bogle Hegarty)

GLOBAL LOYALTY

The newly revitalised
Executive Club means
it's now even easier for
members to travel the world

The British Airways Executive
Club frequent flyer programme
was refreshed as part of the 2011
£5 billion business plan. Since its
launch in 1982 it has become one of
the most successful customer loyalty
programmes, with four membership
tiers offering major benefits regardless
of what ticket price customers
have paid. An integral part of the
British Airways brand family, its
reward currency, renamed 'Avios', is
also the currency for all loyalty and
reward programmes owned by IAG,
including Iberia Plus and Airmiles.

Above: 'Home Advantage' was the name of the UK advertising campaign used during the period of the London 2012 Olympic and Paralympic Games to drive home British Airways' customer promise 'To Fly. To Serve.' The subtle theme was 'Don't Fly', that is, with the Olympic Games on one's doorstep what better than to attend and cheer on the participants, whatever their nationality. British Airways would more than benefit from the millions of overseas visitors expected to descend upon the UK for the duration of the event. (Bartle Bogle Hegarty)

Right: Airport lounges are just one of the benefits enjoyed by Executive Club members. The Galleries First lounge in Heathrow's Terminal 5 is a luxurious, quiet haven in which to relax pre-flight. (Bartle Bogle Hegarty)

DISTINCTIVE
SERVICE

The value-added extras that make
BA's award-winning short-haul
service the best in class

Rolled out in 2014, a new Club Europe seat and cabin interior is the latest product improvement as part of British Airways' £5 billion business plan, and is a clear signal that the short-haul European market remains a key component. The redesign very much reinforces the premium nature of British Airways as a brand, even on short-haul routes, and also emphasises the overall style and experience across the airline's European products no matter what the customer pays. Distinctive service and those value-added extras, the 'frills' if you like, make British Airways' award-winning short-haul service the best in class. (Bartle Bogle Hegarty)

This and next page: The Airbus A380 and Boeing 787 are the most recent additions to the British Airways fleet – part of its £5 billion business plan investment in planes, products and, critically, its people. Like any great customer-focussed brand, how its people perform will determine if its customers' expectations are being met and the new aircraft will be a considerable help. (Right: Bartle Bogle Hegarty, next page: Airbus)

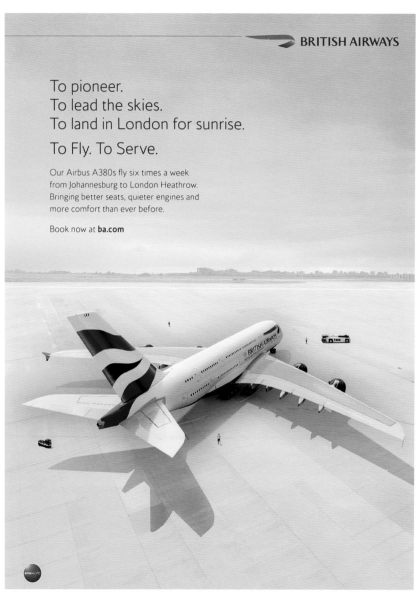

EXPERTISE

RICH HERITAGE

EXCELLENT SERVICE

'To Fly. To Serve.' is now the consistent manifestation of the airline's brand promise to perform, a simple message that clearly says what British Airways and its people stand for in putting their customers at the heart of their business. 'Welcome to British Airways.'

9

BETTER BY DESIGN

In the eyes of the travelling public, the British Airways brand has been shaped both by advertising and experience – from great ads to great apps, an evolutionary trend currently taking the best of new technology and blending it with great service. A common thread has been continual improvement and innovation, along with the recognition that great journeys begin well before the aircraft takes off and continue after it lands. That recognition itself has shaped British Airways' forty years of progress and redefined air travel into the twenty-first century.

Great design has been an integral part of that journey, and now the company is striving for the perfect balance in creating the best travel experiences with the least environmental impact. The new focus on responsible air travel has considerably raised the profile of design.

To be a leader is about creating more with less but still with style and requires emotion, warmth and a character of purpose within the limitations that an air journey inevitably brings. The new design challenge is to deliver the ultimate journeys in the most responsible way and deliver the premium experience people expect of British Airways.

This all adds up to making not just the travel experience but also the customer feel special: a careful combination must be created of British style, thoughtful service and flying know-how – those three distinctive pillars referred to earlier that have shaped the British Airways brand and provided the foundation for its promise to deliver each and every time. Such attention to detail has created that emotional connection that keeps customers coming back. It's what makes a great airline better; in British Airways' case, better by design.

Opposite: Great advertising continues to entice and shape travel preferences as it has always done. The messages are not so very different over the decades but the march of technology and changing society inevitably influence style and presentation. From the skill of the artist to that of the photographer and digital art worker, great ads ignite a passion to travel and great prices make it happen. They are an integral part of shaping the British Airways brand. (Bartle Bogle Hegarty)

BRITISH AIRWAYS

SURPRISING FLORIDA

Florida Fly Drives.
Flights + 7 days car hire
from £479pp.
Plus hotel offers.
Book by 30 April
at ba.com

1800 miles of coastal road
and many more exotic
species. We fly to Orlando,
Tampa and Miami daily.
To Fly. To Serve.

BRITISH AIRWAYS **AVIS** Car Rental in Partnership with **VISIT FLORIDA.** oneworld

TODAY IN GRENADA
33°c
7 NIGHTS ALL INCLUSIVE FROM
£949 pp

Today's live temperature from the
Met Office makes Grenada one of
the world's warmest destinations.
For more great offers go to ba.com

To Fly. To Serve.

GRENADA
The Spice of the Caribbean

BRITISH AIRWAYS

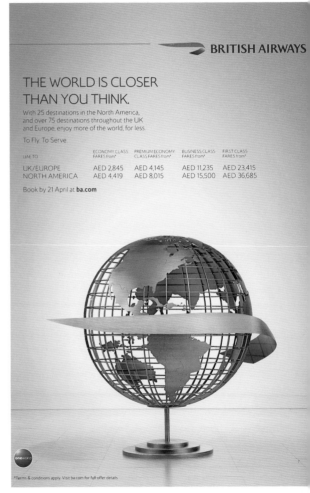

BRITISH AIRWAYS

THE WORLD IS CLOSER THAN YOU THINK.

With 25 destinations in the North America,
and over 75 destinations throughout the UK
and Europe, enjoy more of the world, for less.

To Fly. To Serve.

UAE TO	ECONOMY CLASS FARES from*	PREMIUM ECONOMY CLASS FARES from*	BUSINESS CLASS FARES from*	FIRST CLASS FARES from*
UK/EUROPE	AED 2,845	AED 4,145	AED 11,235	AED 23,415
NORTH AMERICA	AED 4,419	AED 8,015	AED 15,500	AED 36,685

Book by 21 April at **ba.com**

oneworld

From drawing board to on board: delivering the ultimate journeys in the most responsible way. (Bartle Bogle Hegarty)